CUBE
BOOK

SKY

WHITE STAR PUBLISHERS

TEXTS BY

MAURIZIO BATTELLO

ARIEL BRUNNER

LUCA MERCALLI

RICCARDO NICCOLI

CARLOS SOLITO

JASMINA TRIFONI

project manager and editorial director
VALERIA MANFERTO DE FABIANIS

editorial coordination
GIADA FRANCIA

graphic design
CLARA ZANOTTI

editorial staff
ENRICO LAVAGNO

translation
CATHERINE BOLTON
MARESA MOGLIA

© 2006 WHITE STAR S.P.A.
VIA CANDIDO SASSONE, 22-24
13100 VERCELLI - ITALY
WWW.WHITESTAR.IT

ISBN 88-544-0124-2

REPRINTS:
1 2 3 4 5 6 10 09 08 07 06

Printed in Singapore
Color separation: Chiaroscuro, Turin

CONTENTS

SKY

1 • A storm unleashes itself on Colorado State, U.S.A.

2-3 • Lightning plays over the plains of Alberta, in Canada

4-5 • Late at night, the sun "sets" in Finland.

6-7 • In a surreal vision balloons crowd the sky over Albuquerque, New Mexico.

8-9 • *Frecce Tricolori* in action at Foggia, Italy.

11 • In Sweden, cirrus and cumulus clouds are colored by the setting sun.

13 • Under a cover of storm clouds, the day's light dies away.

14-15 • Cosmic rays color the Finnish night.

16-17 • The beginning of the rainy season in Australia.

18-19 • Dawn on the Bosque del Apache NWR; New Mexico.

20-21 • A tornado approaches the fields of Colorado.

Introduction

by Jasmina Trifoni

EVER SINCE HUMANS STARTED TO ROAM THE PLANET, THE HORIZON THAT SEPARATES NEARBY EARTHLY THINGS FROM THE INACCESSIBLE WORLDS BEYOND HAS BEEN THE BACKDROP FOR ALL OUR ACTIVITIES. THE SKY HAS INSPIRED GENERATIONS OF POETS AND PAINTERS, PHILOSOPHERS AND SCIENTISTS. ITS TAPESTRY OF STARS HAS GUIDED NAVIGATORS. THROUGH THE VIOLENT FORCE OF STORMS AND HURRICANES, THE SKY HAS BROUGHT TERRIFYING MENACES AND TERRIBLE DESTRUCTION, AND THE DARKNESS OF SOLAR ECLIPSES HAS BORNE THE TROUBLING MESSAGES OF ANCESTRAL DEITIES. THE SKY HAS MARKED HARVESTS WITH THE CONSTANT CHANGING OF THE SEASONS, CELEBRATED OUR ROMANCES WITH ITS

• Lovers of paragliding in the Netherlands are at the mercy of the same forces and elements that create a glorious backdrop of clouds and sun rays.

Introduction

FIERY SUNSETS, AND BUOYED OUR DREAMS WITH THE SUDDEN ARC OF A FALLING STAR.

WITH ITS UNFATHOMABLE MYSTERIES, THE SKY HAS ALWAYS HELD IRRESISTIBLE CHARM FOR US. INDEED, STARTING WITH THE MYTHICAL ICARUS, THE MOST EXTRAORDINARY MEN AND MINDS HAVE ATTEMPTED TO REACH, CONQUER AND CONTROL IT. LEONARDO DA VINCI SPENT YEARS DESIGNING HIS FLYING MACHINES, AND PHILOSOPHERS HAVE TURNED TO THE HEAVENS TO CREATE THEIR NOTIONS OF THE COSMOS.

ON 9 OCTOBER 1604 GALILEO WAS GAZING AT THE SKY WITH HIS TELESCOPE WHEN HE SUDDENLY SAW A *STELLA NOVA* APPEAR: THE IMMUTABLE SKY OF THE ANCIENTS WAS

Introduction

NEVER THE SAME AGAIN. OVER THE CENTURIES, THROUGH THE INVENTION OF NEW INSTRUMENTS, WE HAVE DISCOVERED THAT TREMENDOUSLY VIOLENT EVENTS TAKE PLACE OUT THERE, MILLIONS OF LIGHT-YEARS AWAY FROM US. WE HAVE LEARNED THAT STARS ARE BORN AND DIE, ENDING THEIR LIFE CYCLE WITH MAJESTIC EXPLOSIONS THAT LEAVE BEHIND SPECTACULAR CLOUDS OF DUST, CELEBRATING THE ETERNAL DANCE OF MATTER.

AND NOW THAT WE HAVE FINALLY LEARNED TO FLY, IN MANY WAYS THE SKY IS NO LONGER THE SACRED AND INVIOLABLE ELEMENT IT WAS FOR OUR ANCESTORS. WE CROSS IT, OUR NOSES GLUED TO THE WINDOWS OF AN AIRPLANE, ADMIRING THE LANDSCAPE THAT BELOW US STRETCHES FOR

Introduction

ENDLESS MILES. THE ADVENTURE OF SPACE TRAVEL HAS EVEN ALLOWED US TO VIEW OUR PLANET SWATHED IN THE UNMISTAKABLE BLUE GLOW THAT MAKES EARTH A UNIQUE SPECTACLE IN THE SOLAR SYSTEM. BUT WHAT IS THE SKY? WHERE DOES IT START AND WHERE DOES IT END? IF WE THINK ABOUT IT, THE SKY DOESN'T REALLY EXIST. WHAT WE CALL THE SKY IS SIMPLY THE ILLUSION OF THAT SUBTLE AND INTANGIBLE WINDOW WE CALL THE ATMOSPHERE, WHICH SEPARATES US FROM THE UNKNOWN AND FROM THE BOUNDLESS SPACES OF A TURBULENT, UNKNOWABLE UNIVERSE. AND YET, THE VERY FACT THAT IT DOESN'T EXIST MERELY ADDS TO THE INTRIGUE OF THE MULTIFACETED EXPANSE ABOVE US.

27 • Orderly rows of stratiform clouds announce the sunset over Africa's savanna.

28-29 • Minor swans take flight in Cambridgeshire, England.

30-31 and 32-33 • Acrobatics and technology at high altitudes: sky surfing in France and flying over the Everest massif (Nepal-China) for documentary purposes.

THE SKY FROM THE SKY

LUCA MERCALLI

- Seen in a spectacular satellite shot, vast disturbances hide the Java Sea.

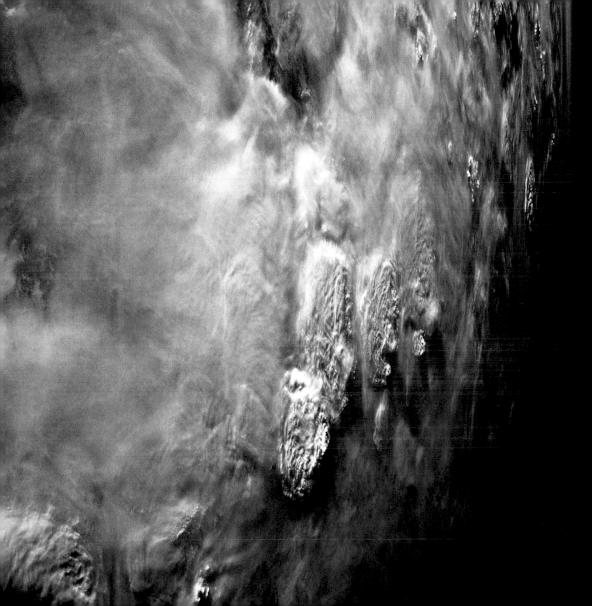

INTRODUCTION The Sky from the Sky

Viewed from space, Earth is a blue planet dotted with white bubbles and whorls: oceans and clouds. Apart from the deserts, the planet's landmasses are dark and inconspicuous. Man's first opportunity to observe the sky from space came on 1 April 1960, when America's National Aeronautics and Space Administration (NASA) sent history's first weather satellite, TIROS-1, into orbit. However, these satellite images were fuzzy, black-and-white pictures that needed to be reassembled to form mosaics of photographs. Initially, the simple television camera on board could only operate in daylight, but instruments were then introduced in order to produce infrared images at night. The Rus-

INTRODUCTION The Sky from the Sky

SIANS LAUNCHED THEIR FIRST WEATHER SATELLITE IN 1969. THIS MACHINE, WHICH WAS BORE THE CHILLY NAME METE-OR-1, REPRESENTED THE LEGACY OF KNOWLEDGE AC-QUIRED OVER YEARS OF EXPERIMENTATION – FOR EXAM-PLE, WHEN YURI GAGARIN GAZED DOWN AT THE EARTH'S HEAVENS IN ALL THEIR MARVELOUS AND EXTRAORDINARY UNIQUENESS ON 12 APRIL 1961, DURING MAN'S FIRST BRIEF FLIGHT INTO SPACE. NEIL ARMSTRONG, EDWIN (BUZZ) ALDRIN AND MICHAEL COLLINS GOT A MUCH BETTER VIEW OF THE SKY ON 20 JULY 1969, WHEN THEY SET FOOT ON THE MOON. TODAY, SCIENTISTS AND METEOROLOGISTS CONTIN-UOUSLY OBSERVE THE SKY FROM SPACE. THE SKIES – WE SHOULD USE THE PLURAL FORM, AS THERE ARE SEVERAL – ARE ANALYZED, FILTERED, PHOTOGRAPHED, FILMED AND

The Sky from the Sky
Introduction

SCANNED IN DETAIL. NUMEROUS SATELLITES AND ORBITING STATIONS GIVE US A CONTINUOUS FLOW OF IMAGES THAT WE CAN SEE ON TELEVISION AND COMPUTER SCREENS, A PRIVILEGE WE OFTEN UNDERESTIMATE. SEEN FROM ABOVE, EARTH'S SKY CHURNS WITH THE ROUNDED PEAKS OF EQUATORIAL THUNDERCLOUDS AND WHIRLS WITH THE VAST, SPIRALING DISTURBANCES OF THE MIDDLE LATITUDES. THIS SILENT VITALITY IS WARMED BY THE HEAT OF THE SUN, AND SHIFTED BY THE WINDS AND CONDENSING WATER DROPLETS. ONLY FROM SPACE CAN WE UNDERSTAND THE FRAGILITY OF OUR ATMOSPHERE: VIRTUALLY ITS ENTIRE MASS IS CONCENTRATED IN A LAYER THAT IS JUST 12 MILES THICK, A THIN SKIN THAT SEPARATES LIFE FROM EMPTINESS.

- Outside the *Discovery*, Mark C. Lee and Carl J. Meade test the Simplified Aid for EVA Rescue (SAFER), a device for the individual recovery of astronauts "lost" in space.

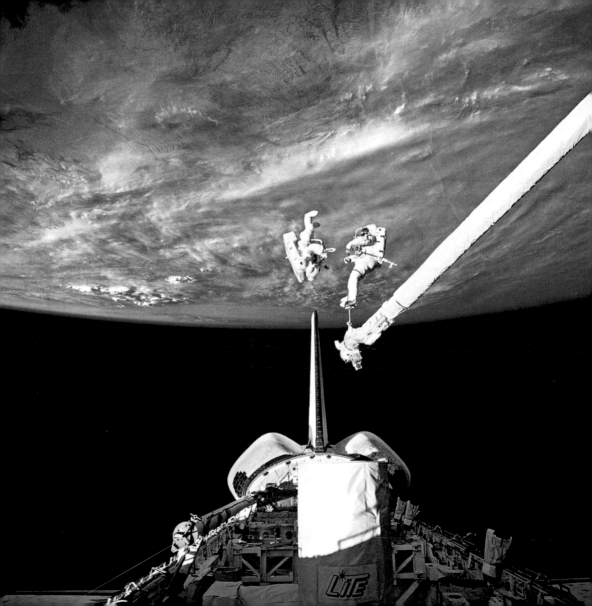

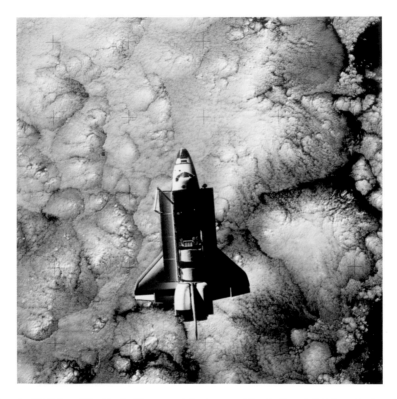

40 • In 1995 the *Atlantis* shuttle completed seven trips to Russia's Mir orbital station.

41 • Story Musgrave and Donald Peterson working on maintenance aboard the *Challenger*.

42 ● The *Atlantis* was given this name in honor of the first American oceanographic research ship.

42-43 ● The *Endeavor*, which was built to replace the *Challenger*, was first launched in 1992.

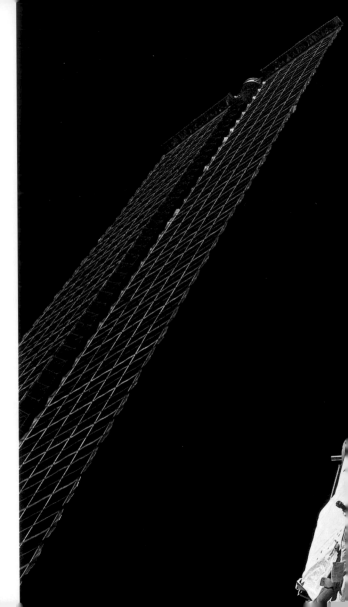

Astronaut Michael Lopez-Allegria working on the International Space Station (ISS) during a session of extravehicular activity (EVA).

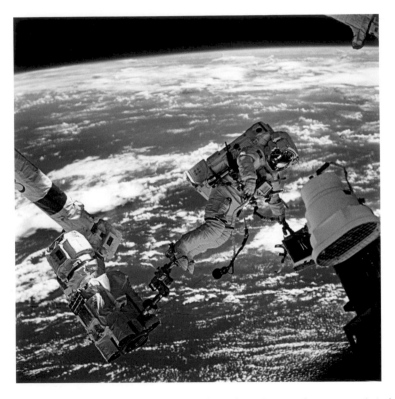

46 • An astronaut, firmly strapped into the Canadarm 2 extension, proceeds to install observation devices.

47 • NASA astronauts are busy repairing the Hubble space telescope.

48 • The *Magellan* probe is ready to free itself from the *Atlantis* and to head
toward Venus for radar exploration.

49 • A smiling Valery Polyakov looks out from the porthole of the Russian space station
Mir during its encounter with the *Voyager* shuttle, in February 1995.

● These images, made against the background of the intricate clouds that cover the earth's surface, clearly depict the International Space Station.

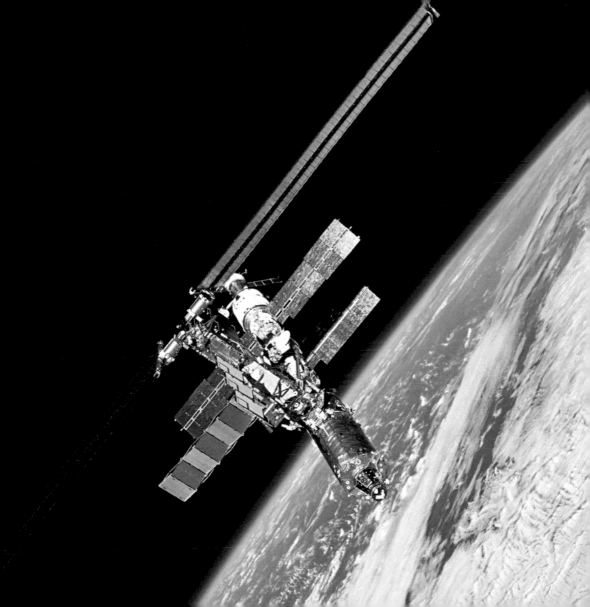

52 • A break in the clouds reveals Isla de Guadalupe, in the Pacific Ocean.

53 • Enormous cumulonimbus tower over the Pacific filmed by the *Discovery*, whose verticle stabilizer is visibile above.

54 • A cyclone begins to develop over the Atlantic Ocean.

55 • In September 1985, armed with all its destructive potential, Hurricane Elena moved toward the Florida coast.

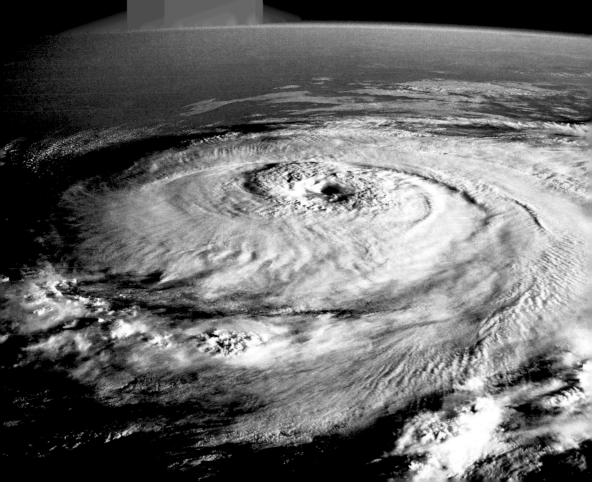

56 • A mass of cumulonimbus threatens South America.

57 • Iniki was one of the most devastating hurricanes in the history of the U.S.A. and certainly the most violent to strike Hawaii.

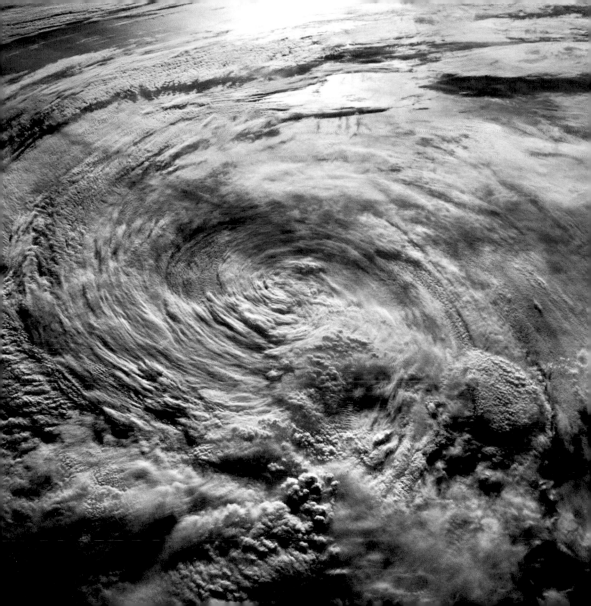

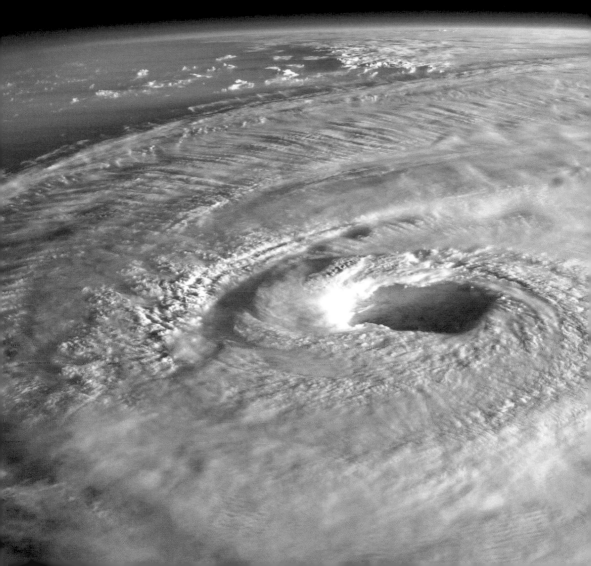

September 2003:
Hurricane Isabel, which
developed over the
Atlantic Ocean, west of
Cape Verde, moves
toward the Caribbean
and the Bahamas.

In this 2003 photograph, the eye of Cyclone Isabel is clearly visible within an area of low pressure, where temporary calm reigns, foreboding renewed violence.

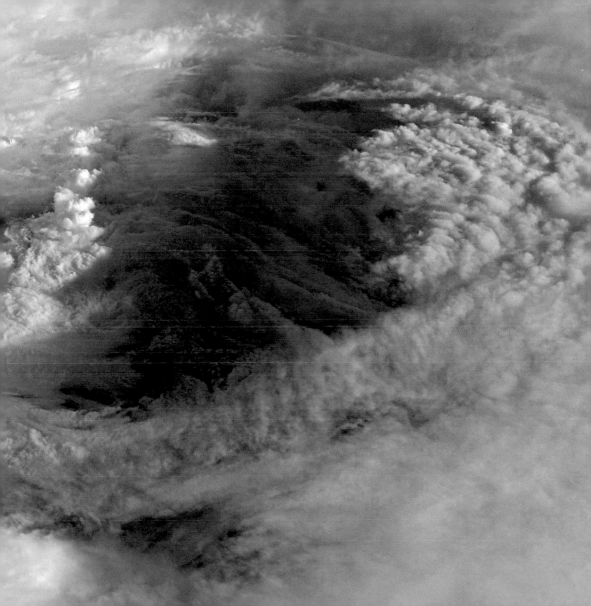

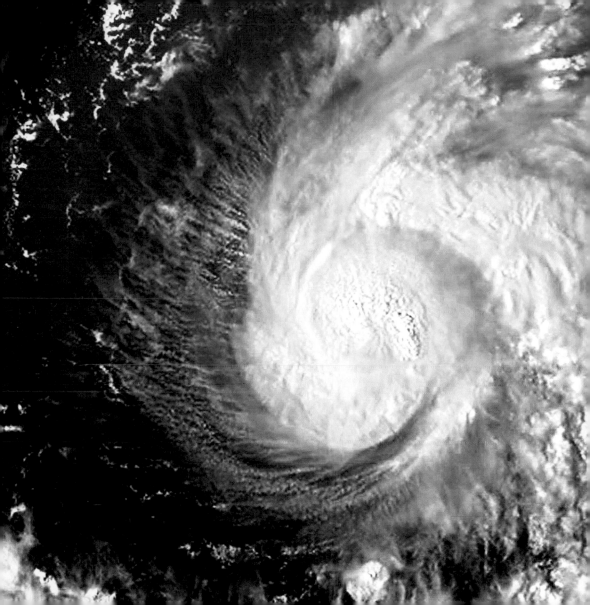

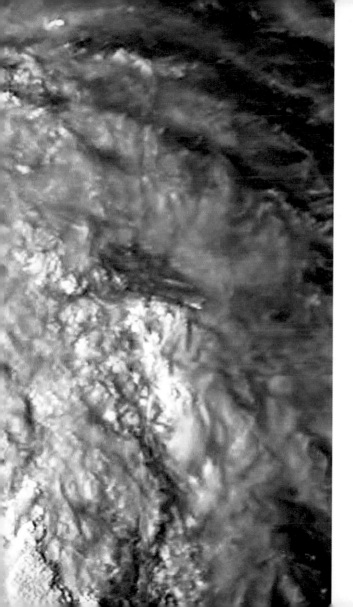

In September 1999 Hurricane Floyd moved toward the Lesser Antilles, causing heavy rain and strong winds along most of the Atlantic coast.

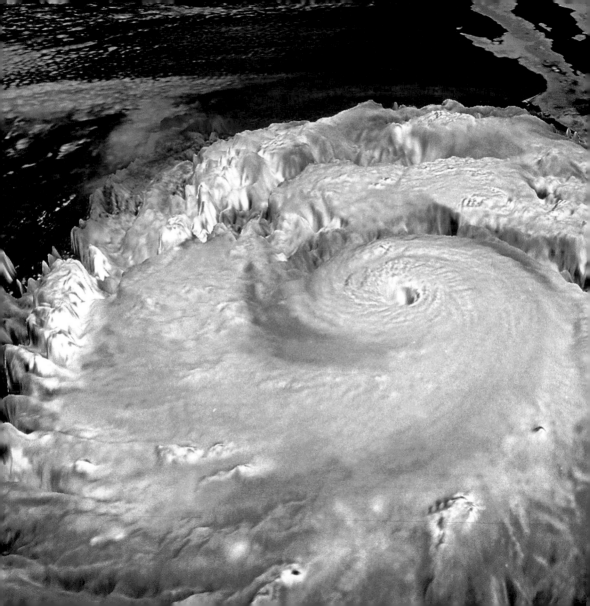

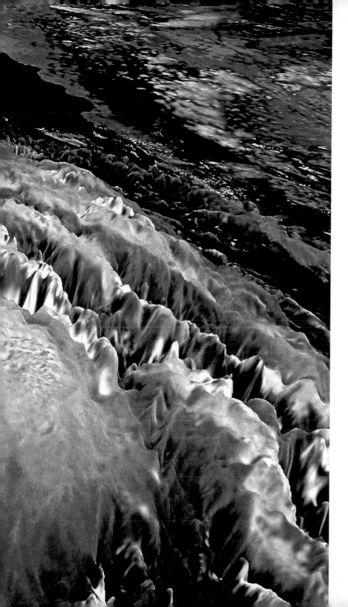

A hurricane strikes the coast of Baja California (at top of photograph). "Hurricane" derives from "Hurican," a Caribbean god of evil.

A sequence of three images shows the evolution of Hurricane Andrew, which in August 1992 devastated the Bahamas, Florida and the Gulf of Mexico, dying out in Louisiana.

In august 1999, the tentacular hurricane Dennis begins as a tropical depression in the southeastern Carribean, gaining the violence of a hurricane as it reaches the Hispaniola island. At the lower right corner Cuba is visibile.

Two devastating hurricanes approach America's east coast, with the Greater Antilles and Florida visible in the two images: Floyd (left) in September 1999 and Isabel (right) in September 2003.

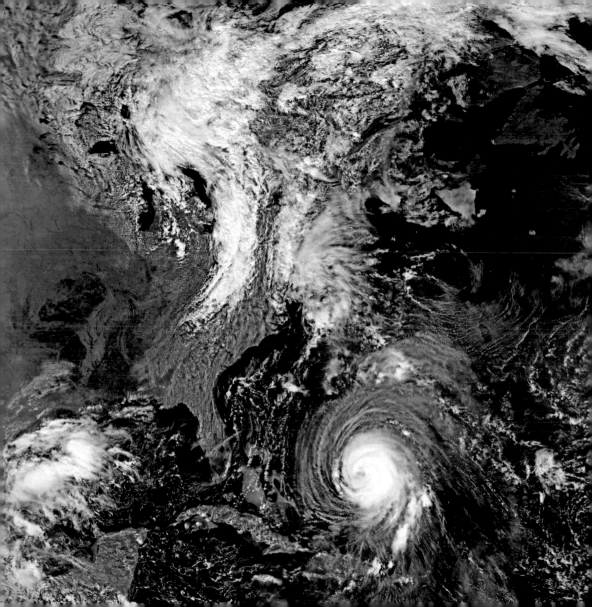

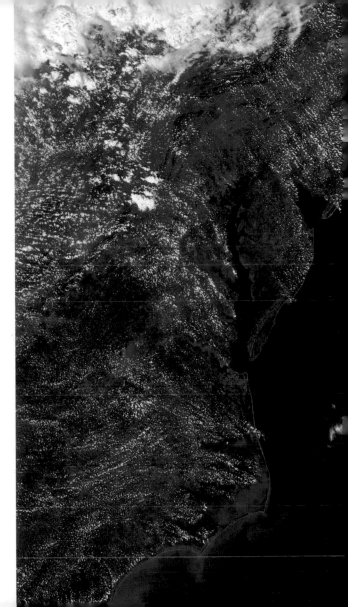

● Hurricane Alex, in 2004, travels at 18 miles (29 km) per hour, with whirling winds of over 93 miles (150 km) per hour. The area shown extends from North Carolina (bottom) to Boston, Massachusetts (top).

Photographed from a the satellite, Earth often appears to be composed only of oceans and clouds, as in these two images shot over the Pacific Ocean.

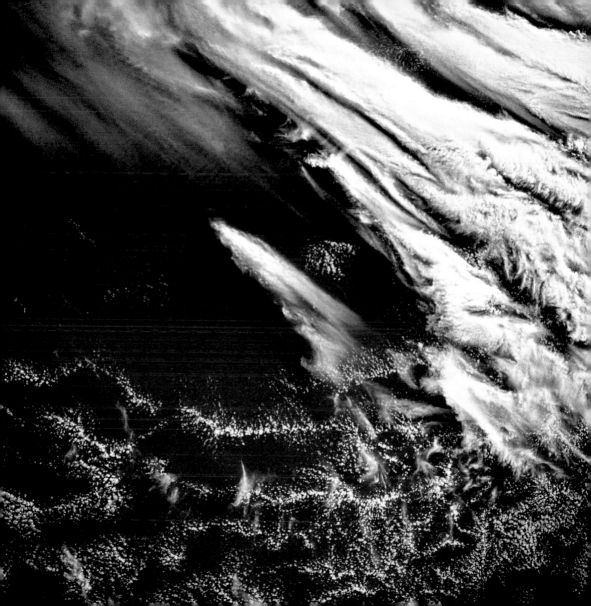

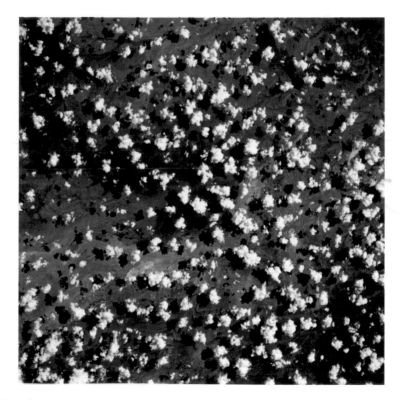

76 • Sparse clouds (*cumulus humilis*, heralds of good weather) move slowly over the River Giuba, Somalia's principal waterway.

77 • Dense clouds seem to perform a circular dance over the Isla de Guadalupe.

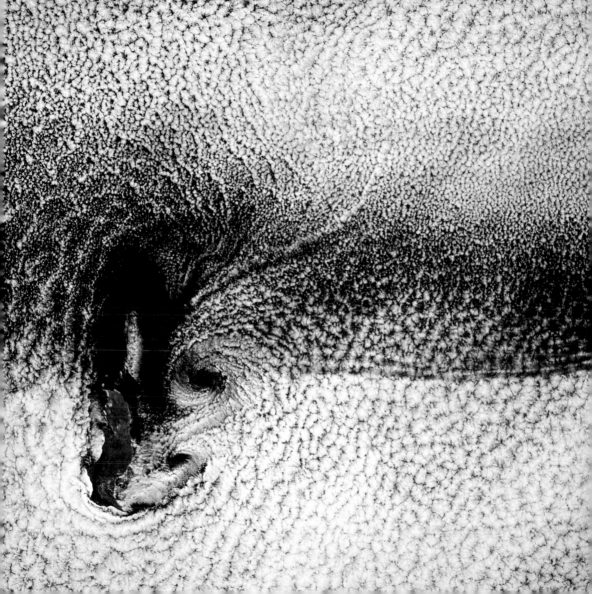

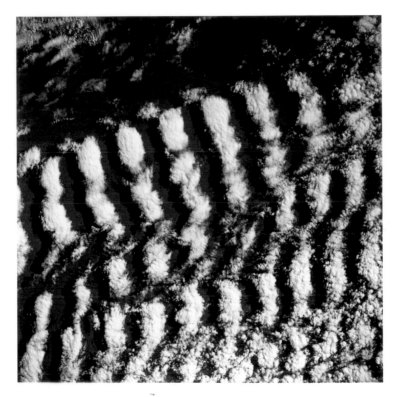

78 • Formations of stratocumulus clouds photographed by the *Discovery*, cross the Australian desert.

79 • Tempestuous high-altitude winds create thick formations of clouds on the mountain peaks of Western Australia.

80 • Cloud formations extend for miles over the Pacific Ocean.

81 • On its route across the Pacific Ocean, a ship produces a wake of condensation.

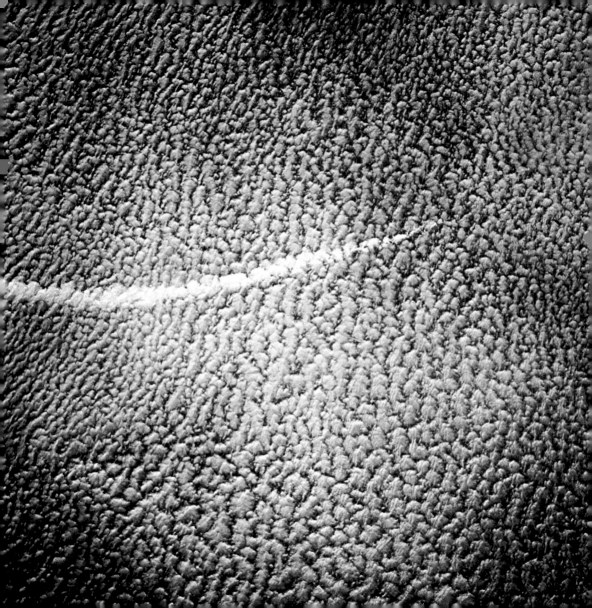

BREWING STORMS

LUCA MERCALLI

- A "supercell," the most dangerous type of storm, rages over the state of Kansas.

INTRODUCTION Brewing Storms

In THE *ODYSSEY* ULYSSES' JOURNEY WAS DOTTED WITH TEMPESTS THAT TURNED THE SKY LEADEN AND UNLEASHED THE IMPETUOUS WINDS FROM THE BAGS AEOLUS HAD GIVEN HIS CREW. SHAKESPEARE NAMED ONE OF HIS COMEDIES *THE TEMPEST,* AND A SEA TEMPEST INSPIRED ONE OF VIVALDI'S CONCERTOS. AND THERE ARE TEMPESTS IN VERGA'S *THE HOUSE BY THE MEDLAR TREE* AND MELVILLE'S *MOBY DICK.* THERE ARE MOVIE STORMS CREATED USING COMPUTERS AND SPECIAL EFFECTS, LIKE IN *THE PERFECT STORM,* BASED ON THE BOOK BY SEBASTIAN JUNGER.

THERE ARE STORMS OF ALL KINDS: WIND, SNOW, RAIN AND SAND. TEMPESTS, GALES, HURRICANES, SQUALLS, CY-

- Lightning rents the night sky above Pueblo, Colorado: its light is equivalent to 100 million lightbulbs.

INTRODUCTION Brewing Storms

CLONES AND TORNADOES ARE DIFFERENT WORDS USED TO DEFINE THE EFFECTS THAT THE VIOLENCE OF ATMOSPHERIC EVENTS HAS IN THE SKY AND ON LAND, SEA AND EVEN ON THE HUMAN SPIRIT. THERE IS ALSO A SCALE – THE BEAUFORT WIND SCALE – THAT SPECIFIES THE APPLICATION OF THESE WORDS. WINDS MUST BLOW AT A SPEED OF LEAST 55 MILES PER HOUR TO MERIT THE TERM "STORM." BELOW THAT, IT IS CONSIDERED A "GALE." ASIDE FROM CLASSIFICATIONS, HOWEVER, DARK SKIES CROSSED BY AIR FUNNELS OR SWEPT BY WINDS ARE ALWAYS AN ORDEAL FOR HUMANS, PLANTS, ANIMALS AND EVEN THE LAND, AS THEY ERODE, CARRY AWAY OR PILE UP SAND OR SNOW, AND CHURN UP THE SEAS. THERE ARE VAST AND ENDURING STORMS AS WELL AS SHORT LOCALIZED ONES.

INTRODUCTION Brewing Storms

THE VAST AND ENDURING STORMS, LIKE LOTHAR AND MARTIN, ARE ASSOCIATED WITH DEPRESSIONS IN THE MIDDLE AND NORTHERN LATITUDES. FROM DECEMBER 25 TO 27, 1999 THESE TWO STORMS HIT THE ATLANTIC COAST OF FRANCE AND THEN BATTERED SWITZERLAND AND GERMANY WITH WINDS OF UP TO 155 MPH, LEAVING BEHIND NUMEROUS VICTIMS, AS WELL AS DOWNING TREES AND POWER LINES. OTHERS ARE CLASSIC SUMMER STORMS, WHICH HIT SUDDENLY WITH GUSTS OF UP TO 95 MPH AND CLOUDBURSTS, HAIL, THUNDER AND LIGHTNING. STORMS CAN TURN INTO TORNADOES, LIKE THE FAMOUS ONES THAT SWEEP ACROSS AMERICA'S GREAT PLAINS. SOME OF THEM ARE LESS THAN 1000 FEET IN DIAMETER, BUT THEY HAVE THE MOST POWERFUL AND DESTRUCTIVE WINDS ON

Brewing Storms

Introduction

EARTH. DURING ONE OF THESE TERRESTRIAL VIOLENT VORTICES THAT STRUCK ON 3 MAY 1999, A DOPPLER RADAR AT BRIDGE CREEK, OKLAHOMA, MEASURED WIND SPEEDS OF OVER 315 MPH. TROPICAL STORMS – HURRICANES IN THE ATLANTIC AND TYPHOONS IN THE PACIFIC – ARE THE MOST IMPETUOUS ONES. THEY LAST FOR WEEKS AND FOLLOW PATHS CONTINUING FOR THOUSANDS OF MILES, BRINGING HIGH-SPEED WINDS AND TORRENTIAL RAINS, AND DEVELOPING THE COMBINED POWER OF MANY NUCLEAR EXPLOSIONS. THEY HAVE DOCILE NAMES LIKE ANDREW, MITCH, GEORGES AND IVAN, BUT LOOKING THEM IN THE EYE MEANS PUTTING YOUR LIFE IN DANGER.

89 and 90-91 • The hot, humid days often end with impressive storms when the hot, humid land air rises like a big bubble, condensing into a rain cloud.

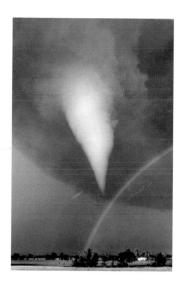

92-93 • A supercell, also called mesocyclone, begins to form the typical "cone" that preceeds the tornado.

93 • The rainbow's graceful presence only renders the twister's tunnel-shaped clouds more terrifying.

● A dreaded twister is about to beat down on Mulvane, in Kansas. This tornado was recorded as an F3 (on a scale of five grades), with winds at 155-185 miles (250-300 km) per hour.

A tornado near Big Spring, Nebraska is about to end its destructive existence.

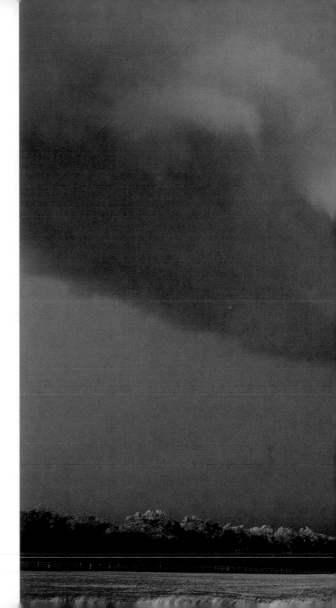

The dust cloud on the horizon is all that remains of a house struck by a slender but devastating tornado: an F3, classified as "severe" on the Fujita Scale.

100 ● The irrevocable hammer blow of a twister is about to strike near Boulder, Colorado.

101 ● The tornado's fearsome trunk is often short-lived (from 1 to 10 minutes),
but the most devastating phenomena can last up to an hour.

The most violent supercells are capable of generating up to four or more tornadoes simultaneously, as here, in Nebraska.

BEHIND STORMS AND LIGHTNING, WE NO LONGER IMAGINE ANGRY, JEALOUS GODS, BUT ARE STILL LEFT WITH A SENSE OF LOSS, AN EMPTINESS THAT FADES ONLY WITH THE PASSING OF THE STORM.

104-105 • In the nucleus of a lightning bolt like this one, the air temperature may rise to 30,000°C.

106-107 • Lightning strikes near Uluru, in Australia, a site sacred for the Aboriginals.

A vast formation of altocumulus clouds creates a singular contrast between the blue sky and the sunset on the horizon of the Masai-Mara National Reserve, Kenya.

110-111 • Heavy rain over Puerto Natales, Patagonia, Chile.

112-113 • Within just a few seconds, these nimbostratus rain clouds unloaded tons of water on this deserted pasture.

114-115 • During the summer (June, July, and August in calendrical terms) the North American Great Plains are subject to violent meteorological phenomena, like this cloud formation photographed over corn fields in Illinois.

116-117 • The lightning that strikes inside storm clouds acts like the filaments inside a lightbulb, creating an impressive natural sight.

118-119 • Pushed upward by hot air in rapid ascent, an enormous cumulonimbus is forming near Liberal, Kansas.

120-121 • A nimbostratus full of rain, which can reach from 9850-16,400 ft (3000 to 5000 m) in thickness, completely obscures the sun, blotting out the landscape.

122-123 • A sea of clouds releases rain farther along Highway 27, South Dakota.

124-125 • A storm, a relatively frequent phenomenon between March and June, hovers over the savanna in Kenya.

126-127 • A summer storm strikes cultivated fields near Ritzville, Washington State.

128 • An isolated thunderstorm approaches the Midwestern plains, U.S.A.

129 • An isolated downpour approaches the monotonous Lano Estacado, between Texas and New Mexico.

130-131 and 132-133 • "Atmospheric monsters" forming over South Dakota and Colorado.

134 and 134-135 • A giant tornado and a
dangerous rotating supercell rage over
central U.S.A.

136-137 • The rain season is heralded
in great style in Australia's Northern
Territory.

138-139 and 140-141 ● Urban areas, probably due to their higher temperatures, seem to attract more storms than rural areas.

142-143 ● A mesocyclone, or "supercell,"strikes Kansas. From these supercells, tornadoes are formed, approximately 800 each year in the USA.

144-145 ● A wall of lightning illuminates the countryside in Hampshire, Great Britain.

146-147 ● Aside from the lightning in this photograph taken in South Dakota) we can distinguish earth-to-cloud bolts, intranimbus (inside the clouds), cloud-to-cloud and cloud-to-sky bolts.

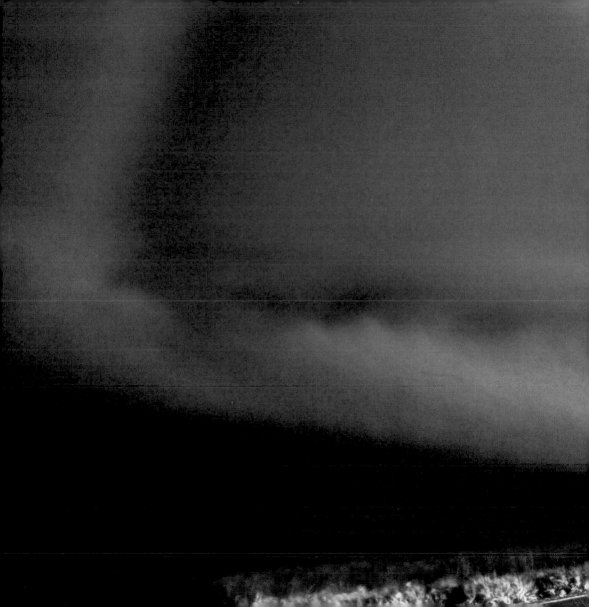

In addition to their destructive winds, supercells, like this one photographed in Kansas, produce and hurl out dangerously large hailstones.

150-151 ● A supercell, nourished by violent ascending currents or updrafts, rages over Nebraska.

152-153 ● The quiet of Custer State Park, South Dakota, is about to be shaken by a summer storm.

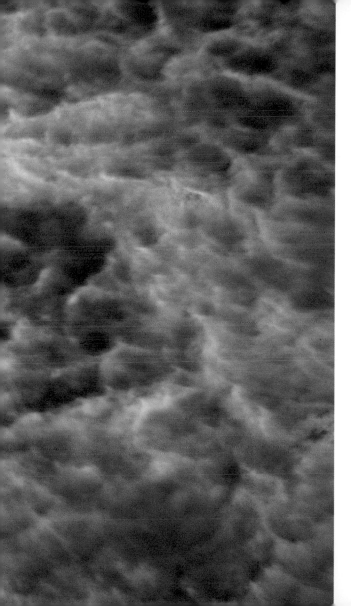

154-155 • The summer monsoon produces roiling cloud filled skies over Angkor Wat, in Cambodia.

156-157 • A supercell, future "mother" of a crop of tornadoes, saturates the atmosphere on a hot Nebraska afternoon.

158-159 • The terrifying scene which this particular storm system produced over El Paso County, Colorado, lasted for over two hours.

160-161 • The light at sunset inflames a storm cloud, creating a hellish scene.

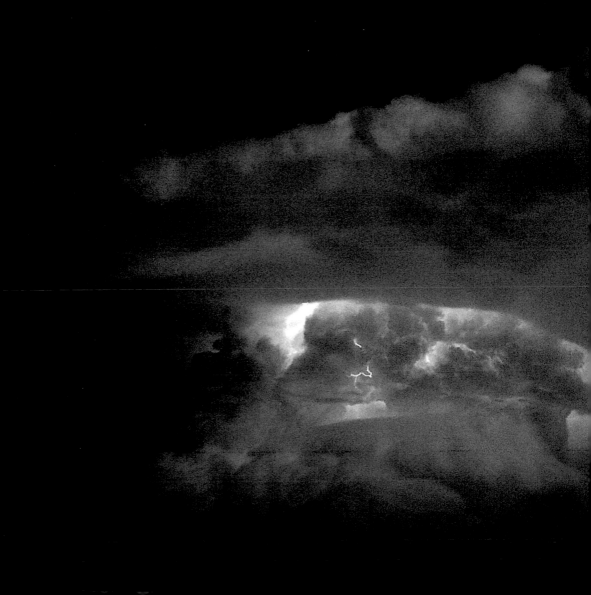

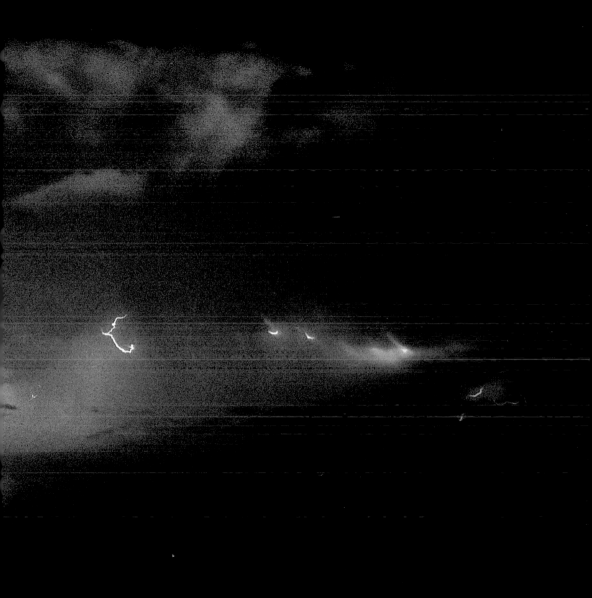

162 ● In a chaos of clouds, the air becomes thick and unstable in the skies of Colorado.

162-163 ● A passing storm, off the coast of Borneo, is about to unload enormous masses of water during its "mature" phase.

164-165 ● Feeble traces of lightning illuminate a column of rain, created by a storm in Colorado.

166-167 ● After striking Baja California, Mexico, a storm that formed in the south of the State, moves toward the Pacific Ocean.

168-169 and 170-171 ● Surrounded by unnaturally still air, the remains of a tornado-forming cloud over Colorado take on strange shapes.

172-173 ● Reassuring rays illuminate the Colorado countryside: the State, subject to about 40 tornadoes yearly, is ninth on the list of the U.S.A.'s most frequently hit zones.

SKIES OVER THE WORLD

JASMINA TRIFONI

- At dawn the Eiffel Tower and the cupola of Les Invalides compete with the luminous Parisian sky.

INTRODUCTION Skies over the World

Which sky is the most famous? Which one has been captured on film most often by tourists from all over the world? Perhaps the dazzling one with a million lights that dominates the unmistakable New York skyline. Or maybe the turquoise sky outlining the austere dome of St. Peter's in Rome on balmy May evenings. Or could it be the dappled azure sky that peeks through the steel girders of the Eiffel Tower in Paris? And which one is the prettiest? The one that stretches over the endless African plains and looks as though it has gently come to rest on golden savannas? What about the sapphire sky that stands out against the bright red of the fragile sandstone monuments

INTRODUCTION Skies over the World

OF ARCHES NATIONAL PARK IN UTAH OR AUSTRALIA'S MA-
JESTIC ULURU – ALSO KNOWN AS AYERS ROCK? OR COULD
IT BE THE FIERY DUSK OF A TROPICAL ATOLL?

WE MAY NOT STOP TO THINK ABOUT IT, BUT THE SKY FOL-
LOWS US WHEREVER WE GO. WE LOOK AT THE SKY TO UN-
DERSTAND WHAT THE WEATHER WILL BE, AND THE SKY IN
TURN AFFECTS OUR MOODS. THE SKY MOVES US WITH
THE MAGIC OF A SUNSET APPEARING UNEXPECTEDLY BE-
HIND A CURTAIN OF LEADEN CLOUDS, SURPRISES US WITH
THE SUDDEN SPECTACLE OF A RAINBOW, SADDENS US
WITH THE DRAB GRAY OF A RAINY DAY, AND FRIGHTENS US
WITH THE UNSTOPPABLE POWER OF HURRICANES, TY-
PHOONS AND TORNADOS.

THE SKY IS THE WORLD'S THEATER, THE BACKDROP OF

Skies over the World

Introduction

EVERY INSTANT OF OUR LIVES. AND YET IT'S MORE THAN THAT, BECAUSE AT THE SAME TIME IT ALSO PLAYS A KEY ROLE IN OUR EVERYDAY LIVES. IT IS A SILENT AND NEGLECTED PLAYER WE OFTEN TAKE FOR GRANTED, BUT ONE WE CARRY WITHIN US. THIS IS WHY WE ALL HAVE A SPECIAL PLACE IN OUR HEARTS FOR THE MEMORIES OF OUR MOST CHERISHED SKIES. THESE ARE THE SKIES THAT HAVE SEEN OUR ROMANCES BLOSSOM AND FADE, THAT HAVE WATCHED US REJOICE AND SUFFER, LAUGH AND CRY. THEY ARE THE SKIES WE HAVE CAPTURED IN THE PHOTOGRAPHS OF AN UNFORGETTABLE VACATION. AND THE ONES THAT HAVE SIMPLY ALLOWED US TO DAYDREAM.

179 ● The red sandstone of Monument Valley, Utah, contrasts with the grey sky at dawn.

180-181 ● Altocumulus clouds glide over the port of Tromso, Norway.

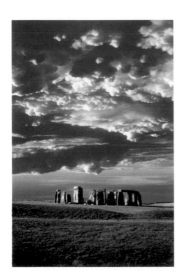

● Predecessor of all celestial
observatories, the famous megalithic site
at Stonehenge has for centuries captured
the imagination of scholars and visitors.

The Callanish Stone Circle, on the western coast of the Isle of Lewis, in the Hebrides, Scotland, dates back to circa 2000 B.C.

The Kremlin's golden
cupolas brighten
Moscow's overcast sky.

188 • The purity of clear Nordic skies, although rare, offers incomparable sensations of vastness, as in this image of the 15th-century St. Olaf's Castle, Savonlinna, Finland, contstructed to protect the realms of Sweden and Finland.

189 • The intense light emphasizes the architectonic volume of the Alcázar in Segovia, Spain.

190-191 • The overcast sky exalts the purity of the pale stone the château of Chambord, reflected in the waters of the River Cosson, in the Loire Valley, France.

Paris' sunsets are perhaps the most famous in the world, with participants like the Seine, Ile de la Cité, and the Notre Dame cathedral.

Dawn's gentle light bathes Frankfurt-on-Main, pride of the new Germany.

Great fireworks illuminate the impressive National Gallery, Prague, (left) and London's Tower Bridge (right), one of the world's most famous.

198-199 • Dawn lights floods the Mount Blanc massif, which dominates the shared borders of France, Italy and Switzerland.

200-201 • A sea of stratus clouds hides the valleys of Trentino-Alto Adige.

Right after a summer rainstorm, the sky clears over Venice, with the church of Santa Maria della Salute in the foreground.

A majestic pyrotechnic night show is held each year in Venice during the celebrations for the Redeemer.

206 and 207 ● With the first light of day, a thick fog clears to reveal the ancient town of Saint Stephan of Magra, in the province of La Spezia.

208-209 ● A stormy sky heightens the harshness of Capraia, in the Tuscan Archipelago, off the coast of Grosseto.

The dense afternoon light increases the grandiosity of the Cathedral of St. Mary of the Assumption, Siena.

212 • Pisa's striking Leaning Tower is confronted with a formation of cirrocumulus clouds.

213 • The Duomo's magnificent lantern stands proudly against the skies over Florence.

214-215 • A shroud of nimbostratus promises rain on Rome's Imperial Forum.

216-217 • Low on the horizon over Rome's famous roofs, the sun creates a suggestive counterpoint with the dome of St. Peter's.

218-219 • Surprising and intense in the first light of day, the ancient city of Piazza Armerina is silhouetted against a stormy sky.

220-221 ● The night sky brings a magical stillness on frenetic Athens and the Acropolis.

222-223 ● The similar forms of the Blue Mosque and St. Sophia contrast with the warm tones of sunset over Istanbul.

224-225 • The top of a building provides an excellent view of a violent storm approaching Mysore, India.

226-227 • A magnificent bridge between earth and sky, this rainbow seems to spring directly from the Potala in Lhasa, Tibet, the ancient winter residence of the Dalai Lama from the 15th to the 20th century.

228-229 • Storm weather builds up over Samye Monastery, Tibet. This image reveals a *chorten* – a Tibetan Buddhist reliquary.

230-231 ● The afternoon light floods the Annapurna massif, in Nepal.

232-233 ● Under a humid sky, the Yarlung Tsangpo, in Tibet, flows toward India.

234-235 ● The spires of Buddhist shrines rise against the sun in Myanmar's Pagan valley.

236-237 ● After a brief but intense summer storm, the sun shines on Chao Phraya River, in Bangkok, Thailand.

238-239 ● The Cambodian forest invades an ancient artificial water basin in the immense temple complex of Angkor Wat.

240-241 ● Monsoon clouds are about to obscure the face of a Khmer monarch at Angkor Thom.

242-243 ● Fluffy clouds have just bathed the center of Shanghai, China, with welcome rain.

244-245 • In a dramatic scene dominated by Mt. Fuji, a Shinkansen bullet train speeds across the Japanese countryside.

246-247 • Ever since its completion in 1886, the Statue of Liberty has been well protected from inevitable lightning bolts.

248-249 • The refined, elegant and historic city of Boston, Massachusetts, illuminated by the setting sun.

260-261 •
A storm at sunset
heightens the colors
in Grand Canyon
National Park.

262-263 •
Suspended between
earth and sky,
Monument Valley's rock
formations rise
majestically in the
Navajo Indian
Reservation, in Utah
and Arizona states.

● A slice of light
enlivens the splendid
Uxmal site, one of
Yucatan's most famous
centers between the
VII and X centuries A.D.

● A compact formation of good weather cumulus (or *cumulus humilis*) clouds, passes over Uluru (Ayers Rock), Australia. Uluru is the second largest monolith in the world after Burringurrah, also in Australia. Both are sacred sites for Aboriginals.

268 and 269 • The sky, with its atmospheric phenomena, is the author of many marvels. They include the Devil's Marbles, giant masses of Australian granite (left); the egg of a legendary serpent that is part of Aborignal mythology; and the fossil dunes near Lake Mungo, Australia (right).

270-271 • Condensed humidity over the Southern Australian Basin creates a narrow but vast layer of clouds on London Bridge, in the waters of Victoria State.

272-273 • The sky, although overcast, rarely brings rain to the Olgas, a well-known Australian range.

274-275 • At dawn, an expanse of clouds meets the ocean along the coast of Victoria State, Australia.

Inevitable morning fog embraces the peaks of Kilimanjaro, between Kenya and Tanzania.

MASTERS
OF THE
AIR

ARIEL BRUNNER

- Seagulls are present at almost all latitudes, wherever there is a stretch of coast on which to nest.

INTRODUCTION Masters of the Air

The flight of birds has captured our attention since the dawn of time. Who can resist the sight of birds soaring across the sky? Embodying a defiance of the force of gravity, they have inevitably fascinated humans, eternally earthbound. The dream of flying is part of every child's fantasies, and it is one of humanity's most recurrent ambitions. Even now that we have become so accustomed to flying, we are still astonished by the swift's daredevil acrobatics and the eagle's majestic glide. The magic of flight has made birds one of our most important symbols. Noah sent a raven and then a dove to find land after the flood, and the dove, returning

INTRODUCTION Masters of the Air

WITH AN OLIVE BRANCH, HAS BECOME THE ETERNAL SYMBOL OF THE QUEST FOR PEACE AND A BETTER WORLD. LIKEWISE, THE EAGLE HAS LONG BEEN THE UNDISPUTED EMBLEM OF POWER.

BUT THE FLIGHT OF BIRDS IS MORE THAN THE SIMPLE DEFIANCE OF GRAVITY: FLYING MEANS TRAVEL. THE ARCTIC TERN, WHICH JOURNEYS EVERY YEAR BETWEEN THE ARCTIC AND ANTARCTICA, AND THE ALBATROSS, WHICH CAN SPEND YEARS WANDERING THE SOUTH SEAS, ARE LIVING MONUMENTS TO THE POWER OF NATURE. BUT SO ARE LITTLE MIGRATORY PASSERINES: THOUGH THEY WEIGH ONLY A FEW GRAMS, THE ONES SEEN IN EUROPEAN GARDENS CROSS THE MEDITERRANEAN AND THE SAHARA EVERY YEAR. THE ARRIVAL

Masters of the Air

Introduction

AND DEPARTURE OF MIGRATORY BIRDS MARK THE SEA-
SONS. BIRDS THUS ACT AS THE MESSENGERS OF TIME,
LIKE THE SWALLOWS AND STORKS THAT ANNOUNCE
THE ARRIVAL OF SPRING TO EUROPEANS. BIRDS SHOW
US THE ELEGANCE OF FLIGHT, BUT THEY ARE ALSO AN
EXTRAVAGANZA OF COLOR AND SONG. WITH THE AVIAN
SPECIES, EVOLUTION HAS PRODUCED SOME OF THE
MOST ELABORATE MUSIC AND HAS PAINTED SOME OF
THE MOST BREATHTAKING PICTURES ON THE PLANET.
THE WARBLE OF A NIGHTINGALE OR GOLDEN ORIOLE
AND THE EXPLOSION OF COLOR OF A FLAMINGO OR
BIRD OF PARADISE REPRESENT THE ART OF NATURE,
ONE OF THE ESSENTIAL JOYS OF LIFE FOR ALL OF US.

- The Andes rise in the backround, while close up,
a condor breaks through the thick clouds.

284 • Opening its webbed feet as if they were an airplane's wheels,
a gannet gets ready to land.

285 • Terns are able flyers, capable of dominating even the most tempestuous winds.

286-287 • Waiting for the storm to break, flocks of gannets dive for the fish
near the water's surface.

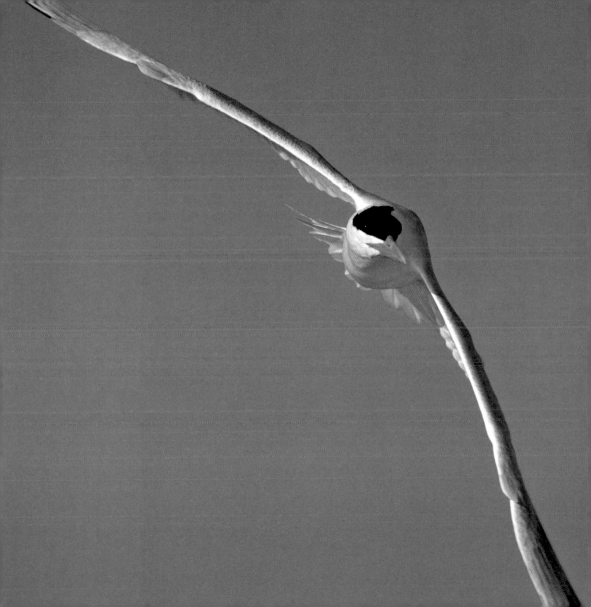

288 • The elegant flight of the terns can be observed in the high latitudes.

289 • Laughing Gulls are recognizable for the black mask around their eyes.

290-291 • A flock of seagulls hovers in the clear sky over the Greek islands, taking advantage of the warm ascending currents.

292 • The elegant tern is a small bird compared to other marine species: its white-feathered wings seldom exceed 27.5 inches (70 cm) when spread.

293 • The Mediterranean skies are a paradise for seagulls who, like kites, let themselves ride on the winds.

294 • The American wood ibis, a member of the stork family, survives in the Florida Everglades.

295 • Using dry grass, a European stork prepares its nest at dizzying heights.

296 • Storks are symbols of good luck in almost all ancient traditions.

297 • The heron makes its home near waterways, weaving together nests of twigs, perched in the tallest trees.

● Swans, with their close relatives the geese, share the habit of long-distance migrations.

Slender and graceful, storks fly elegantly fly over the
Bosque del Apache, New Mexico.

The unmistakable profile of the lesser egret against the blue Mexican sky.

304 • The great white heron lives on the cultivated fields of Europe and North America.

305 • Dancing in the sky, seagulls fight for a small prey.

306-307 • In the light of the tropical sunset, a compact group of pink flamingoes take off, flying low over the ground.

308-309 • Hundreds of starlings take flight at sunset, animating the dull autumn sky.

310-311 • The silent passage of a flock enlivens the autumn sky for a few moments: in this "lethargic" season, the migratory passages offer surprising scenes.

312 and 313 • In rigid V-formation, or flying solo, the snow geese (left) and a bar-headed goose (right) migrate to the warm south.

314-315 • Apparently unfit for flight, geese are actually resistant and capable of facing long flights without resting.

The snow goose is a great flyer. It lives in North America, Siberia, Greenland and some areas of Japan.

318 • The Canadian stork reigns at Bosque del Apache, New Mexico, a reserve founded in 1939 to protect these migratory birds and other aquatic species at risk.

319 • The pink spoonbill, which is gifted with an exceptional wing span, is related to the European stork but lives in South America and the Caribbean Islands.

320 • Small, but a potent flyer and able fisher, an American tern has just conquered its prey.

321 • The big wings of the great white egret are visible in the blue sky of Italy's Po Valley.

322 • The fascinating bos'n bird with its red tail hovers in the warm skies over Midway Island in the Pacific.

323 • A heron takes flight, slowly unfolding its majestic wings.

324-325 • The rapid flapping of wings characterizes the flight of California's *totani semipalmatus*, capable of attaining 40 miles (65 km) per hour.

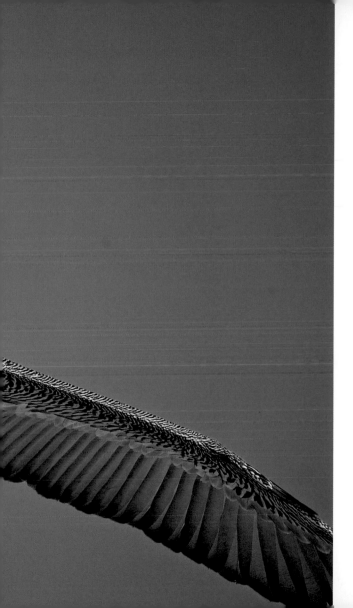

The brown pelican lives on the Atlantic and Pacific coasts, overcoming the winds with strong wings that can reach an 8-ft (2.5-m) span.

328 and 329 • Characterized by long yellow beaks, brilliant bicolor feathers, white pelicans glide through the Mediterranean's tepid air.

330-331 • A flock of pelicans hovers elegantly. Pelicans, although quite heavy, are great flyers and agile swimmers.

66 THE PELICAN'S FLIGHT - CROUCHED, UNGRACEFUL, EXHAUSTING - IS CLOSER TO MAN'S THAN TO THE DELICATE HOVERING OF THE STORKS, OR THE FRENETIC WING-FLAPPING OF SWALLOWS. EVEN THE SEAGULL'S GRACEFUL FLIGHT IS DISTANT: HIGH IN THE SKY, AS EFFORTLESS AS THE WIND OR THE MOVEMENT OF THE CLOUDS. FOR US ,TO CONQUER THE SKY IS A DIFFICULT AND NOT ALWAYS VICTORIOUS CHALLENGE WITH NATURE. 99

Bald eagles use great quantities of energy while hunting and must spend a lot of time resting, which makes it difficult to photograph them in flight.

The bald eagle, with its two and a half meter wing span, is the majestic symbol of the United States of America.

● At high speed, after a 330-ft (100-m) dive, the bald eagle throws itself on its prey, usually a rodent or small mammal.

338 • Feared predator of the European coast, the sea eagle prefers to hunt other birds.

339 • With less than 3.2 ft (1 m) of wing span, a red kite reaches formidable speed in flight, and is capable of dizzying dives.

340 • The Californian condor is recognizable by the intense pink of its head,
which contrasts strongly with its big black wings.

341 • The splendid crowned crane has a characteristic way of flying, with its neck extended,
that distinguishes it from others types of cranes.

● The South African vulture is clumsy on the ground but assumes a noble carriage in flight, thanks to its huge wing span.

344 • The albatross, dominating the coasts, is a strong, able flyer.

345 • A flock of South African seagulls appears off the coast of Dyer Island, South Africa.

346-347 ● A Pacific albatross follows the path of a ship.

348-349 ● Half-closing its eyes to resist the wind of the Falkland Islands, a female albatross watches over her young.

HIGH-ALTITUDE SPORTS

CARLOS SOLITO

- A two-stroke motor assures complete autonomy during take-off and control of a hang-glider, the aircraft most similar to birds in weight.

INTRODUCTION High-altitude Sports

THE WIND BLOWS OVER THE FIELD, THE SAIL OF MY PARAGLIDER SWELLS AND, WITH IT, SO DOES MY ENTHUSIASM. FLYING IS ALWAYS AS EXTRAORDINARILY BEAUTIFUL AS IT WAS THAT FIRST TIME IN THE SOUTHERN APENNINES. WHEN THE HARNESS IS TIGHT AND THE EXCITEMENT IS HIGH, YOU NEED TO CHOOSE THE PERFECT INSTANT TO LET THE WIND PICK YOU UP AND CARRY YOU ALOFT, OVER THE FRIGHTENING VOID BENEATH YOUR FEET THAT REGULATES THE DELICATE BALANCE OF FLIGHT. AND THEN THERE IS NOTHING BUT SILENCE. CARRIED BY THE WHISTLING, WHISPERING WIND LADEN WITH SCENTS STOLEN FROM THE GROUND, YOU STUDY THE SKY AND ATTEMPT TO UNDERSTAND THE BILLOWING CURRENTS, TRYING TO RISE HIGHER AND HIGHER. THEN YOU DESCEND, AND ONCE YOU LAND,

INTRODUCTION High-altitude Sports

YOU LOOK UP TO THANK OUR "THEATER" FOR PERMITTING YET ANOTHER HUMAN FLIGHT. SINCE THE DAWN OF TIME, MAN HAS NURTURED A DESIRE TO BE AIRBORNE; ENCHANTED BY THE SIGHT OF THE FASCINATING AND ELEGANT FLIGHTS OF BIRDS; HE SOUGHT TO UNDERSTAND – AND ATTEMPTED TO APPLY – THEIR SECRETS. IT IS A DIFFICULT BUT NOT IMPOSSIBLE UNDERTAKING, AS DEMONSTRATED BY THE MYTHICAL FLIGHTS OF DAEDALUS AND ICARUS, THE EGYPTIAN GOD KHONSU, THE EXPERIMENTS BY THE VERSATILE LEONARDO DA VINCI, AND THE ATTEMPTS OF PRUSSIAN ENGINEER OTTO LILIENTHAL AND THE AMERICAN BICYCLE MAKERS ORVILLE AND WILBUR WRIGHT. FROM ABOVE, EARTH LOOKS MORE ENTICING; FROM THE SKY THE VANTAGE POINTS ARE MORE SURPRIS-

High-altitude Sports
Introduction

ING. IT DOESN'T MATTER HOW YOU GET THERE. IN PARAGLIDERS, HANG GLIDERS, PARACHUTES, HOT AIR BALLOONS, GLIDERS AND ULTRALIGHT PLANES – ANYONE WHO HAS SOARED THE HEAVENS CAN'T HELP BUT FEEL A BIT LIKE JONATHAN LIVINGSTON SEAGULL. IT IS MARVELOUS TO BE ROCKED BY THE WINDS, RAISED BY THERMALS, AND PUSHED BY DYNAMICS WHEREVER YOU ARE IN THE AIR, WITH AN EXTRAORDINARY VARIETY OF LANDSCAPES AND COLORS BENEATH YOU. IN THE EMPTINESS OF SPACE, THE SKY IS THE REALM OF IMAGINATION, DREAMS AND FREEDOM. INDEED, IT IS NO ACCIDENT THAT SAGAS AND FAIRYTALES HAVE BEEN SET IN THE ENDLESS BLUE DOTTED WITH WHITE CLOUDS.

- To glide through the intense blue sky has always been one of man's most fascinating challenges.

Gliders

• Gliding (in this image, classic gliders in action) was the first form of human "heavier than air" flight, performed successfully in the mid- eighteen hundreds.

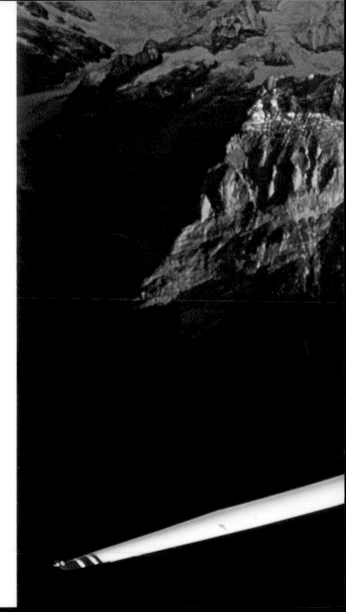

A step beyond the glider is the motorglider, complete with a light propeller 125 hp motor, here photographed in flight over the swiss Alps.

360 • Air acrobatics enthuse glider pilots who today can use dependable gliders

361 • Flying in silence, inside of a heated cabin, makes flight
in a glider a unique experience.

Balloons

362, 363 and 364-365 • Funny alien faces, names of sponsors and colorful flags saturate the sky over Albuquerque, New Mexico, during a famous aeronautic rally.

Preparation for flight in the Namibian desert: the balloon, once inflated, measures approximately 82 ft (25 m) in height and 65.5 ft (20 m) in diameter.

Trips, in a hot air balloon, are interrupted by stops for refueling the gas burner.

● Generally, a volume of aproximately 88,300 cu.ft (2500 cu.m) of hot air is necessary to keep an aerostatic balloon in flight.

Nylon or polyester are the materials generally used to create the balloons, bulbous or of any other shape.

● The simplicity of the aerostatic
concept, the dependability of the material,
and present technology are sufficient to
give any shape to the balloons.

A Halloween pumpkin and a clown peek out of the skies over New Mexico during the Albuquerque International Balloon Fiesta.

- Characters like Mr. Peanut and Mickey Mouse become huge flying figures that catalyze the children's focus on the sky . . . and not only the children's.

• Publicity, on a hot air balloon, lends a touch of "magic," naive but effective.

From fantasy to reality: the duration of a balloon flight varies from 250 to 300 hours.

Parachuting

- Classic canopy shaped parachutes and those with slits are used by the "vintage" parachutists in these photographs, taken between 1969 and 1977.

• Modern "wing" parachutes are similar to air mattresses, rectangular or elliptical according to the flight requirements.

388 • Thanks to the directional cords and stabilizing instruments, modern parachutes are as controllable as small aircraft.

389 • The "parachute pilot," visible in the image, ensures a rapid but smooth opening of the main parachute.

390 • Sport flights with parachutes include interesting choreographies.

391 • Like free falling, sky-divers love aerial acrobatics even during a slow descent with a parachute.

• The great maneuverability of parachutes and the parachutists' coordination and control allows them to create incredibly precise formations.

Acrobatic
sky-diving

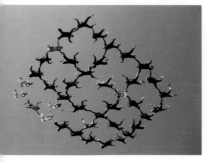

394, 394-395 and 396-397 •
Acrobatic sky-diving requires
many hours of practice.

● With backpacks closed, sky-divers prepare for the moment to open their parachutes, which must take place at a precise height and speed. The security systems often include altimeters that trigger the opening at a certain height, if the diver is unable to do so personally.

● Generally, sport parachute
drops are performed from a
height of 14,700-16,400 ft
(4500-5000 m).

● Spectators are always surprised to witness the relaxed motions of expert sky-divers during free falls.

• Formations vary according to the number of participants: usually 4, 8, or 16, but the record is 300.

406 • During a drop in formation, a group composes the five-rings Olympic symbol.

407 • The capacity for teamwork and individual concentration is no less important than technique during drops in formation.

Sky-surfing

● Sky-surfing exposes the body to the limits of its possibilities, allowing the athlete to move freely in all three spatial dimensions and also in a fourth: relative speed.

● Between the blue of the sky and the cobalt of the Pacific Ocean, air-acrobats playfully challenge the winds.

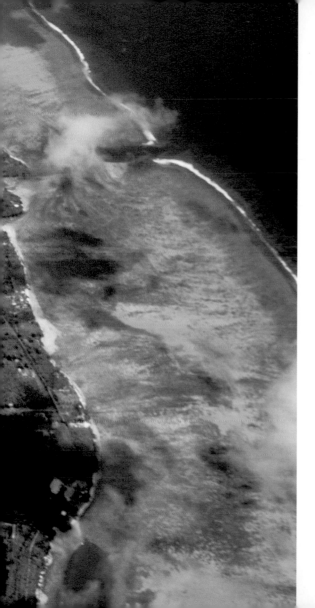

Sky-surfers perform acrobatics over Tahiti's crystalline, transparent waters.

A sky-surfer in action between the sky and the geometric designs of the plains. This type of diving was first performed in France in 1987.

66 **A**IR SPORTS, FROM THE MOST TRADITIONAL PARA-
CHUTISM TO THE AMAZING SKY-SURFING, ARE A MODERN
INVENTION, BUT NATURALLY THE DREAM TO FLY IS ANCIENT.
THE FIRST SUCCESSFUL PARACHUTE DIVE DATES TO THE IX
CENTURY A.D., AND WAS ACCOMPLISHED BY AN ANDALU-
SIAN IN CORDOVA. 99

• The most extravagant acrobatics are probably represented
by the "mirror-image" sky surfing duets

● Patrick De Gayardon and his flights represent a landmark in air sports.

● This is the so-called "relative wind," or air current encountered by sky-surfers that sustains the athletes, permitting the evolutions of this sport.

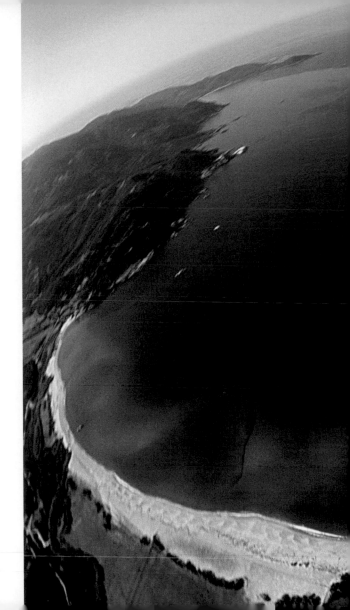

During the final part of the dive, the sky-surfer opens the wing parachute and pulls on the strings to precisely direct his landing.

Sky-diving

- A sky-dive usually lasts little over a minute and is usually done from tourist planes at 13,125 ft (4000 m).

• In free fall, the divers attain 125 miles (200 km) per hour.

• Sky-divers use special suits, according to the type of diving. Those used for relative wind are tight with bootees to cover the space between pant and shoe.

Long free falls require protective headgear because of the high speed at which the divers fall.

Ultralight pendulum

- The name "ultralight pendulum" indicates the peculiarity of these aircrafts: control of the asset and flight path are effected by the pilot by shifting his weight from beneath the wing.

The situation aboard an ultralight pendulum may seem precarious, but these aircraft are actually safe and simple to pilot.

Paragliding

- To determine the direction and speed of the wind is the first step of a paragliding dive.

To avoid collision in flight, there are precise rules of precedence in paragliding.

The scenery for a paraglider varies according to the flight which can, at times, cover many kilometers.

The most natural form of parachuting is paragliding, practiced in mountainous zones.

- The wind speed is fundamental in choosing the moment of the dive. Wind speeds over 12.5-15.5 miles (20-25 km) per hour are excessive for diving.

● After a difficult climb, it's finally time to prepare for a dive off the Swiss Alps.

● Checking on one's psychological conditions before the dive is no less important than checking climatic conditions.

Paragliding can be practiced alone or in tandem (right), a good choice for beginners.

● Nylon antitear fabric with polyurothane to eliminate porosity is the main material of the veil, which weighs approximately 15.5 lbs (7 kg).

A complicated web of cords unites the pilot with the veil, permitting him to modify the shape of the veil in order to perform maneuvers.

Delta-planes

The delta-plane, which has evolved significantly over the last few years, has a direct precursor in the aircraft of Otto Lilienthal, who performed dozens of gliding flights at the end of the 1800s.

458 and 458-459 • Suspended in the baricenter, the pilot commands the delta-plane shifting his weight and acting on the "trapezoid."

460-461 • Support cords strengthen the delta-plane's structure.

California is one of the world's most popular places for open-air sports: the delta-plane attracts many "flyers."

Higher than Mt. Everest: Angelo Arrigo

• In 2003, Angelo Arrigo, winner of many delta-plane event awards, overcame another challenge: flying over the summit of Mt. Everest (right).

466-467 ● Once over the summit of Mt. Everest, Angelo Arrigo came to the Valley of Silence and the Khumbu glacier.

468-469 ● Much more genuine than airplane flight, free flight enacts the ancient dream of human flight with no other support than wings.

THE ART OF CLOUDS

MAURIZIO BATTELLO

- A lentiform altocumulus cloud heralds a storm over Mt. Cook National Park, in the New Zealand Alps.

INTRODUCTION The Art of Clouds

POETRY AND SONGS, PAINTINGS AND LITERATURE – AND EVEN AD CAMPAIGNS AND POLITICAL CONVENTIONS – HAVE USED OR EXPLOITED CLOUDS. WHATEVER THE REASON, CLOUDS HAVE INTRIGUED ALL THOSE WHO ARE SENSITIVE TO THE CONCEPTS OF THE INFINITE AND THE ETERNAL, AND THEY CAST A SPELL RIVALED ONLY BY THE MYSTERY OF LOVE ITSELF. CLOUDS – WHICH ARE SIMPLY WATER VAPOR THAT COMBINES WITH ATMOSPHERIC PRESSURE, ELECTRICAL CHARGES AND AIR CURRENTS – FASCINATE US WITH THEIR SILENT AND EVER-CHANGING DAILY PRESENCE. AS CHILDREN, HOW MANY OF US HAVE STRETCHED OUT ON A LAWN TO GAZE AT THE SKY, ENVYING THE FREEDOM AND SPEED OF WIND-FILLED CUMULUS CLOUDS OR TRYING TO

● A cumulonimbus cloud swells over Las Animas County, Colorado.

FIGURE OUT WHAT THEIR SHAPES RESEMBLE? PEOPLE HAVE EVEN USED CLOUDS TO TRY TO FORECAST THE WEATHER AND CHECK THE VERACITY OF THE PROVERB "MARE'S TAILS AND MACKEREL SCALES MAKE TALL SHIPS TRIM THEIR SAILS." PASSION AND ADMIRATION INSPIRE MANY TO STUDY THE TYPES OF CLOUDS, THEIR FEATURES AND STRUCTURES, AND EVEN THEIR "PERSONALITIES": CIRRUS, ALTOSTRATUS, CUMULONIMBUS, ALTOCUMULUS, CONDENSATION TRAILS (OR CONTRAILS) AND CHEMICAL TRAILS, RARE CUMULUS MAMMATUS CLOUDS, AND THE SIMPLE, LONELY CUMULUS HUMILIS. CLOUDS ARE CLOSELY LINK TO GEOGRAPHY AND COMPLEMENT THE LANDSCAPE. THERE ARE COUNTLESS EXAMPLES: THE CHANGEABLE NATURE OF SCOTTISH CLOUDS HEAVY WITH ATLANTIC RAINS,

INTRODUCTION The Art of Clouds

THE SYMBIOSIS BETWEEN CLOUDS AND IRELAND'S GREEN-ERY, CLOUDS THAT APPEAR TO BE SO LOW IN THE SKIES OF THE CANARY ISLANDS THAT THEY SEEM CLOSE ENOUGH TO TOUCH, THE CLOUDS HOVERING OVER VOLCANIC ICELAND, THE SEEMINGLY FREE-SPIRITED CLOUDS VISIBLE OVER AMERICAN PARKS AND THE STRETCHES OF THE PATAGON-IAN PAMPAS, THE ASTONISHING TOWER CUMULUS CLOUDS OF THE CARIBBEAN, THE TORNADOES OF THE YUCATÁN, THE SUDDEN STORMS THAT BREAK OUT NEAR THE MAG-NIFICENT IGUAÇU FALLS OR THE AMAZONIAN JUNGLE, THE SPIRITUAL CLOUDS THAT SWATHE TIBET AND ARE EN-TWINED WITH THE LOCAL RELIGION, THE COLORFUL CLOUDS OF NORTHERN EUROPE AND, LASTLY, THE DREAM-LIKE CLOUD PATTERNS OF THE *AURORA BOREALIS*. WITH A

The Art of Clouds
Introduction

BIT OF LUCK – AND AN ATTENTIVE EYE – WE WILL DISCOVER THAT CLOUDS OFFER US AN ARRAY OF SHAPES, LIGHTS, COLORS AND OPTICAL EFFECTS LIKE HALOES AND RAINBOWS, REFRACTIONS AND CORONAS. CLOUDS DESERVE CLOSER STUDY AND RESPECT, BECAUSE THEY HELP US EXAMINE THE RAPPORT BETWEEN MAN AND NATURE, FATHOM THE FEAR OF DEATH AND FACE THE MYSTERY OF THE DIVINE. A SENSE OF INVOLVEMENT AND INDIAN WISDOM ARE ESTABLISHED WITH CLOUDS: THEY INVITE US TO PONDER THE SMALLNESS OF HUMANS IN THE SCHEME OF THINGS, HELPING US REALIZE THAT WE ARE PART OF THE PLANET AND THAT WE MUST WORK WITH OTHER CREATURES TO STRIVE FOR A "GENTLE" WAY OF LIFE.

- An altocumulus cloud, unleashing a rainstorm, visible as a diaphanous column at the base of the cloud, on the saline plains of Etosha Pan, in Namibia, Africa.

Described as "fish shaped," lentiform clouds, here photographed in southern Georgia on the U.S.A.'s Atlantic coast, make for one of the most beautiful spectacles that the sky offers, although they often announce bad weather.

480 • A pink light illuminates the inside of an cumulonimbus cloud passing over Colorado.

481 • At over 20,000 ft (6000 m), looking toward the earth, the sky seems like a sea of clouds, formed by the tops of cumulonimbus, altostratus and altocumulus clouds.

482-483 • The "towers" of a congested cumulus rise above the eastern plains of Colorado.

Altocumulus and cirrocumulus, the true sheep-shaped rain clouds are rather similar but form at different heights: the first between 9840 and 20,000 ft (3000 and 6000 m), the second between 20,000 and 36,000 (6000 and 11,000 m).

486 ● Like cotton balls drenched with water, the cirrocumulus float and come apart at high altitudes.

487 ● An impressive bank of cirrus flies high over the Atlantic Ocean, west of Portugal. The photograph was taken from the space shuttle *Challenger*.

488-489 ● At dawn, altocumulus clouds usually offer the most beautiful sights.

490 • Cirrus clouds, at different heights, create a unique pattern.

491 • A bizarre spiral of cirrus cloud is formed by currents at high altitudes.

492-493 • Above 20,000 ft (6000 m) the sky is very often serene with occasional cirrus clouds to whiten the blue expanse.

494-495 ● A tower of cumulonimbus full of rain move rapidly over Kenya's savanna.

496-497 ● Swollen with humidity and electricity, a mass of unstable air advances over eastern Colorado.

The characteristic "cauliflower" form of the cumulonimbus can reach over 6.2-9.3 miles (10-15 km) in height from its base to its top.

While the storm rages, a cumulus cloud begins to dissolve in its upper section.

High-speed air currents "flatten" an cumulonimbus cloud, often the carrier of persistent rain.

Similar to immense wings, low stratiform clouds proceed in a row over the plain.

Strong winds create the suggestive shape of a lentiform altocumulus cloud, characteristic cloud of significant heights, above Mt. Etna.

508, 509 and 510-511 • Sunset makes the clouds' differences in altitude more evident; the rays color the low clouds red and orange, leaving the high clouds in full light.

512 • Clouds of the mammatus (in Latin, "possessing breasts") type, at the edge of a cumulonimbus cloud, move over Boulder, Colorado.

513 • Differences in wind speeds at different altitudes has created a surprising parachute-shaped cloud over Pueblo County, Colorado.

514 • Strong winds form a particular cumulus cloud, herald of storms.

515 • Capricious air currents divide, in a curious fashion, the upper part of a cloud.

516-517 • Altocumulus clouds converge at sunset over Agathe Beach, Oregon..

518-519 • Cumulonimbus clouds appear over this Australian forest, announcing intense storms.

520 ● A magnificent variety of clouds, from isolated low storm cumulus ones to vast extensions of altocumulus ones at higher altitudes, dominates Simpson Bay, in the Dutch Antilles.

521 ● Regular rows of cirrocumulus clouds seem to reflect themselves in the meticulous division of the grain fields in Hill County, Montana.

522 • Once in contact with the limits of the troposphere, at 40,000-42,650 (12,000-13,000 m), a towering cumulonimbus over Costa Rica begins to flatten at its top into the classic anvil shape.

523 • Because of their even, round shape some lentiform clouds, like this one over Huerfano County, Colorado, are often photographed, mistaken for flying saucers.

524-525 • Rippled,
like the surface of the
sea underneath, a vast
bank of clouds floats
over the island of Skye,
in Scotland.

526-527 • Fairy-like
glows form when the
sun, low on the horizon
and protected by low
cumulus and status
clouds, reflect its rays
onto higher clouds, as
seen here here off the
coast of Belize.

Lentiform altocumulus clouds reddened by the sun dominate small cumulus clouds on the peaks of the Parque Nacional Los Glaciares, in Patagonia, Argentina.

530 ● A fiery red cumulonimbus cloud rises near Bothell, Washington State, U.S.A. These clouds appear dark at the bottom, due to their thickness.

531 ● A huge cumulus cloud disintegrates over central Colorado, while the humidity contained within is released as rain, appearing as a veil at the base of the cloud.

532-533 ● Peculiar atmospherical phenomena can create strangely shaped and repetitive clouds, like this one.

534-535 ● A great storm cloud dominates Pueblo County, in Colorado.

536-537 ● Stratified lentiform altocumulus have formed over Tioga Pass in California's Sierra Nevada. These clouds are between 1650 and 4900 ft (500 and 1500 m) thick.

538-539 ● Waving airflows of the wind along the earth's parallel axis sometimes form near mountain ranges, as here in Colorado, forming beautiful twisted clouds, very dangerous for airplanes.

540-541 ● Curtains of high clouds (cirrus and cirrostratus), dispersed in various directions by the winds at different altitudes, color the sky of Michigan over Lake Superior, Michigan.

542-543 ● The sunset illuminates fluffy altocumulus clouds that have released their rain.

544-545 ● The wind, at 9850-13,000 ft (3000-4000 m) gives form to a vast row of lentiform altocumulus clouds over South Island, New Zealand.

The wind, at 3000-4000 meters gives form to a vast row of lentiform altocumulus over South Island, New Zealand.

548-549 • Near Topeka, Kansas, a suggestive expanse of cumulonimbus cloud of the mammatus type follows the wake of storms.

550-551 • Tempestuous mammatus clouds together with the setting sun create a dramatic scene over Avondale, Colorado.

SPECIAL EFFECTS

JASMINA TRIFONI

• In the Antarctic, the *aurora borealis* or "southern lights" takes on the hazy and fascinating shapes of long luminous tails that arise from the ice.

INTRODUCTION Special Effects

As our ancestors took shelter in caves, huddled in the pale glimmer of firelight, nightfall would take them by surprise, bringing with it the threat of predators. One man of the group may have stood guard at the mouth of the cave, keeping watch as his companions slept. This must be how people first began to gaze at the night sky, track the slow cycle of the moon's phases, and wonder why stars twinkle overhead. Thousands of years ago, people used their imagination to group the stars in geometric figures, arranging their mythological gods, heroes and animals in the heavens. And they began to interpret heavenly events as premonitory signs. In addition to the ex-

INTRODUCTION Special Effects

TRAORDINARY SPECTACLE OF THE MILKY WAY, STRETCH-
ING ACROSS THE STARRY HEAVENS ALL THE WAY TO THE
HORIZON, THE NIGHT SKY HOLDS AN ARRAY OF PHENOME-
NA THAT ARE VISIBLE TO THE NAKED EYE BUT WERE INEX-
PLICABLE FOR THOSE ANCIENT OBSERVERS: FROM THE
METEOR SHOWERS WE REFER TO AS SHOOTING STARS, TO
COMETS, THE SOUTHERN AND NORTHERN LIGHTS, LUNAR
ECLIPSES AND THE VIOLENT EXPLOSIONS OF SUPERNOVAS,
WHICH WERE FIRST DOCUMENTED SHORTLY AFTER THE
START OF THE CHRISTIAN ERA AND WHICH FOR CENTURIES
WERE THOUGHT TO REPRESENT THE BIRTH OF A NEW
STAR. ALONGSIDE SCIENTIFIC PROGRESS, THE ADVENT OF
ASTRONOMICAL INSTRUMENTS AND THE WORK DONE TO
PERFECT THEM – CELEBRATED TODAY BY THE PHOTO-

Special Effects
Introduction

GRAPHS TAKEN BY THE HUBBLE SPACE TELESCOPE – HAVE ALLOWED US TO PENETRATE THE SECRETS OF THE SKY AND PLUMB THE OBSCURE DEPTHS OF THE COSMOS. THE NIGHT SKY IS NOT THE SAME AS IT ONCE WAS – AND THIS IS ESPECIALLY TRUE FOR CITY DWELLERS, WHO CAN NO LONGER ADMIRE IT BECAUSE OF THE INVASIVENESS OF ARTIFICIAL LIGHTS. THIS IS A SKY WE HAVE COME TO KNOW WITHOUT FEAR, THE SKY WE USE AS A BACKDROP TO PROJECT OUR LIGHT SHOWS, FROM FIREWORK DISPLAYS TO CLOUD LASERS. THE FIRMAMENT IS NO LONGER THE COMPANION OF UNSHELTERED NIGHTS. BUT PERHAPS THIS IS THE VERY REASON THAT, EVERY SO OFTEN, WE STILL GAZE UP AT THE STARS IN WONDER.

- Among the "special effects" the sky offers, the full moon (here enlarged by a telescopic lens) is the most common, but observed each time with renewed wonder.

A "flaming" aurora, in sinuous movement, over Canada.

● The extraordinary *aurora borealis* mixes its colors with the orange arctic sunset, in the Lakes Region, in Finland.

A tempest of colors, the Scandinavian aurora seems like a pyrotechnical show.

564 • Born of the solar wind, the polar aurora assumes the most varied colors and forms.

564-565 • Auroras are more intense, like this one photographed in the Norwegian skies, during magnetic storms caused by sun spots.

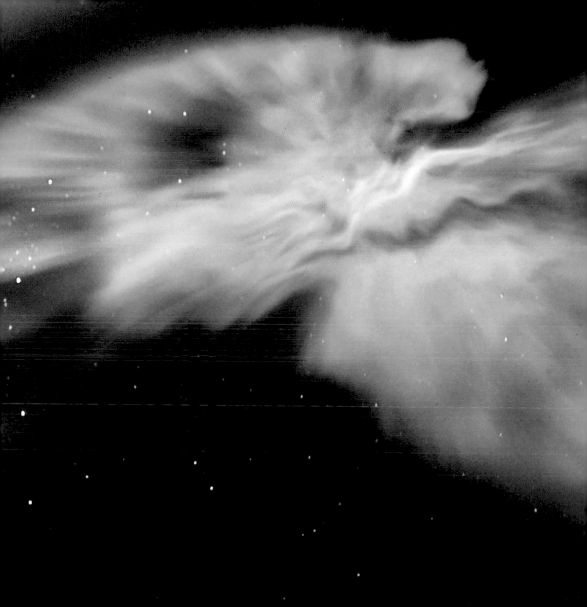

566 ● Like fingers of a pale hand, the filaments seem to rest on the Canadian forests.

567 ● A giant white spiral materializes over a Canadian forest.

568-569 ● Water drops trapped beneath cumulonimbus clouds illuminate the colors on the Cassiar Mountains, in the Yukon.

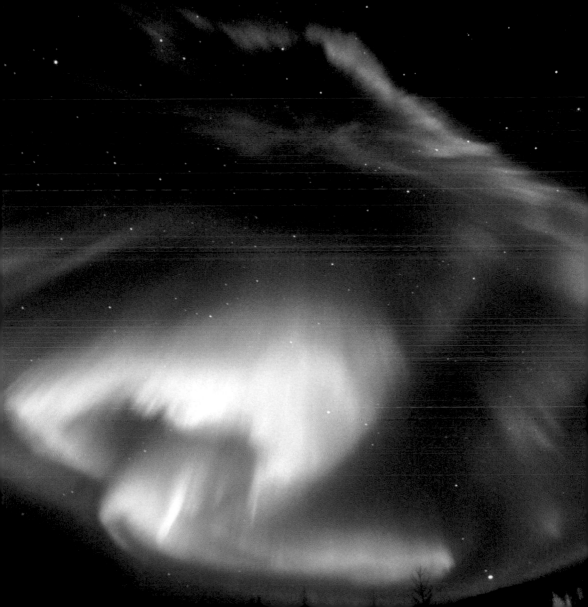

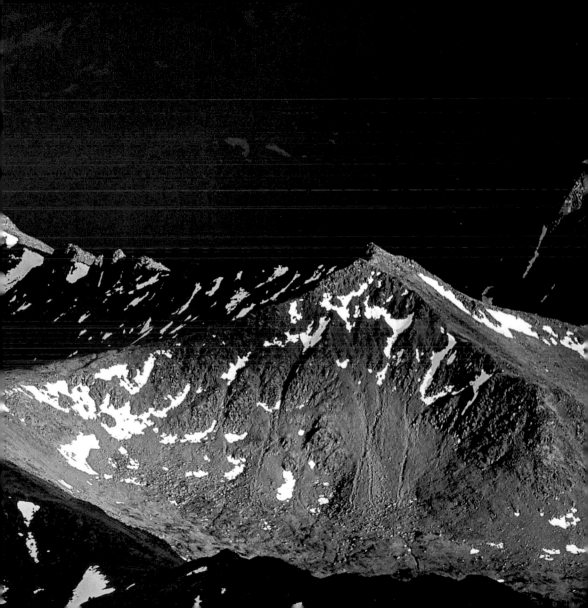

The light spring rain reflects the last rays of the sunset, forming a spectacular rainbow over the Russian steppe.

A play of light and color embrace a bay in the Fjords, South Island, New Zealand, where rain and sea foam meet a sun ray, creating a splendid rainbow.

574-575 and 575 • Unusual rainbows form on the Atlantic (left) and in a high altitude cirrus cloud (right).

576-577 and 578-579 • An enormous rainbow and a singular low arch shine over the continental United States and the Hawaiian island of Maui.

580-581 • The rainbow is a common phenomenon, but is visible only if the sun is lower than 42° in the sky.

582-583 • The spectacle offered by Canyonlands National Park, in Utah, is most impressive when framed by a rainbow.

584-585 • A primary rainbow, clear and complete, is reflected in Jackson Hole, Wyoming.

586-587 • Lentiform clouds, colored by the sunset undermine the moon in the Mediterranean skies.

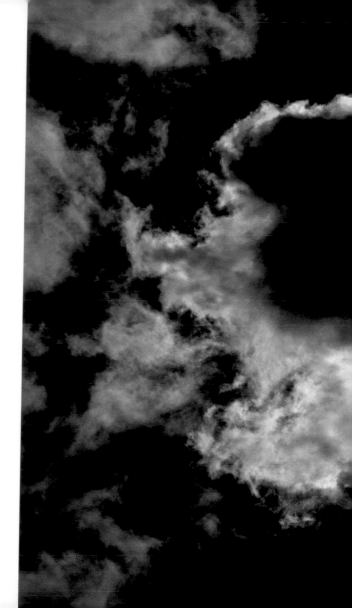

588-589 ● Full moon night: the satellite's light is intense enough to penetrate the clouds.

590-591 ●
The moon's luminosity, diffused by particles of ice at high altitudes and by clouds lower down, spreads over Mt. Denali, Alaska.

592 • A distant divinity, Selene sends her bluish rays on the Sahara desert, revealing the sand dunes.

593 • Beyond the highest peaks of the Alps, in the sidereal frost, our satellite is about to pass from its three-fourth's phase to full moon.

Lens open and
pointed to the north:
the result – a whirlwind
of stars with a focus
on one of the stone
arches of Arches
National Park, in Utah.

LOFTY ACROBATICS

RICCARDO NICCOLI

- With the French flag in the background, the Patrouille de France divides into two formations.

INTRODUCTION Lofty Acrobatics

Acrobatic flying is one of the most rewarding ways to enjoy the complete sense of freedom conveyed by soaring the heavens. Nothing offers more intense physical and visual emotions than hurtling through the air, experiencing the dimensions of space and overcoming the force of gravity like a dolphin leaping and diving in crystal waters. In civil aviation, acrobatic flying – both as a competitive sport and purely for fun – is almost exclusively an individual discipline, but in the military sector it has become a fully-fledged spectacle, with performances by formations composed of numerous aircraft.

INTRODUCTION Lofty Acrobatics

AERIAL ACROBATICS TOOK OFF SHORTLY BEFORE WORLD WAR I, WHEN FLYING MEANT CONSTANTLY RISKING ONE'S LIFE. IT WAS A DARING EXERCISE THAT DEVELOPED DURING THE WAR AS A FIGHTING TACTIC INTENDED POSITION ONE'S PLANE BEHIND THE ENEMY'S IN ORDER TO DOWN IT.

THE ACROBATICS PERFORMED IN BIPLANES AND TRIPLANES SUBSEQUENTLY BECAME TRAINING EXERCISES, FIRST OF ALL TO SELECT THE BEST PILOTS, AND THEN TO ALLOW THEM TO PUSH THEIR PLANES TO THEIR VERY LIMITS IN ALL THREE DIMENSIONS OF SPACE.

DURING THE TWENTIES, THE FIRST FIGHTER FORMATION OF WHAT WAS THEN THE ROYAL ITALIAN AIR

INTRODUCTION Lofty Acrobatics

FORCE CREATED GROUP ACROBATICS. AT THE TIME, THE MAIN PURPOSE OF THIS EXERCISE WAS TO IN-STILL MUTUAL TRUST IN THE YOUNG PILOTS. THE FIRST FIGHTER FORMATION WAS BASED AT CAMPO-FORMIDO, NOT FAR FROM THE CURRENT HEAD-QUARTERS OF THE NATIONAL ACROBATIC SQUAD OF THE FRECCE TRICOLORI.

THE PEOPLE OF THE FRIULI REGION QUICKLY BECAME ACCUSTOMED TO WATCHING THE MAGNIFICENT MA-NEUVERS PERFORMED BY FORMATIONS OF 4 OR MORE BIPLANES FLYING CLOSE TOGETHER TO DESIGN AN AR-RAY OF DIFFERENT FIGURES. IN SHORT, THE FIRST OFFI-CIAL ACROBATIC SQUADS WERE SOON FORMED, AND

INTRODUCTION Lofty Acrobatics

STARTING IN 1930 THEY BEGAN TO PARTICIPATE IN AER-
IAL EVENTS AND COMPETITIONS IN ITALY AND AROUND
THE WORLD. FOLLOWING WORLD WAR II, THE CON-
CEPT OF MILITARY ACROBATIC FLYING IN FORMATIONS
SPREAD AROUND THE WORLD. SHOWCASES OF THE
JOY OF FLYING AND INSTRUMENTS OF WAR ADAPTED
TO PROVIDE ENTERTAINMENT AND DAZZLE STARRY-
EYED CHILDREN, ACROBATIC SQUADS – THE *FRECCE
TRICOLORI* FIRST AND FOREMOST – NOW ASTONISH
CROWDS ALL OVER THE WORLD WITH THEIR BREATH-
TAKING MANEUVERS, EXPERTLY PERFORMING A MIX OF
TECHNIQUE, IMAGINATION, SKILL, PRECISION AND CAL-
CULATED RISK.

Italy

602 • The "Frecce Tricolori" exhibit against a typical British sky
at Fairford, Gloucestershire, U.K., in 2002.

603 • The "Great Wing" is the difficult concluding figure of the Italian "Frecce Tricolori"
exhibition.

● In their Aermachs
MB339A/PANs, the
"Frecce Tricolori"
complete the "Fan"
figure.

- In the "Great Wing" the squad must fly at the slowest speed possible without loosing contact among themselves.

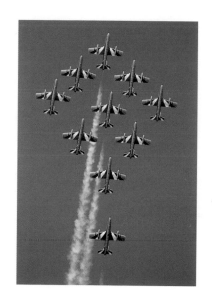

608 • The "Frecce Tricolori'" ten MB.339°/PANs photographed during their vertical flight up into the sky.

609 • The "Bomb" is a famous acrobatic figure Italian pilots invented in the 1930s.

610 • The *Frecce Tricolori* execute a spectacular crossover of the in the skies over Kecskemét, Hungary, in 2003.

611 • Before beginning the "Cardioide," the *Frecce Tricolori* separate vertically into two formations.

612-613 • The *Frecce Tricolori'* white wakes mark the beginning of the "Bomb," while from underneath, the soloist rises toward the center of the figure.

● Two moments of a nose-up in the formation, which leaves
a large white wake in the sky.

France

616, 617 and 618-619 • The Patrouille de France, composed of eight Alpha jets, is performing three classical figures from the repertory: respectively, "Le tonneau en té," "Le diamant dos" and "Le Shérif."

620-621 and 621 ● The Patrouille de France photographed as the pilots fly over Monaco (left), and the Arc de Triomphe (right).

622-623 ● The Patrouille de France inaugurates the 2003 exhibition season in La Vendée.

Spain

624 • These two CASA C.101s of Spain's Patrulla Aquila seem to touch for one moment during this crossover.

625 • The two CASA C.101s of Spain's Patrulla Aquila are flown by trainee pilots.

Switzerland

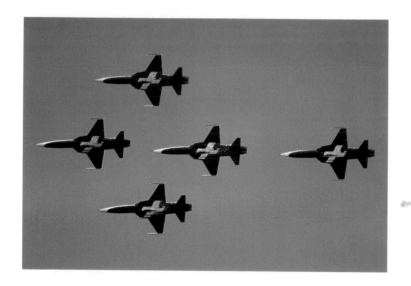

626 • Swiss precision is confirmed by the exhibitions of the Patrouille Suisse, which flies Northrop Hunter F-5Es.

627 • Since 1994, the Patrouille Suisse has performed with six Hawker Hunters.

United Kingdom

- The Red Arrows (formed in 1964) includes a selection of the Royal Air Force's best acrobatic pilots. During their exhibitions they fly the powerful, agile BAE Systems Hawk T. Mk.1.

● Two images of the Red Arrows taken in the leaden skies of the Royal International
Air Tattoo 2002, at Fairford.

A formation of four Hawks of the Red Arrows photographed during take-off; the distance between the aircraft is less than 10 ft (3 m).

- The Red Arrows' crossovers and the nose-up at the limits of the possible have made them famous worldwide. Here they are flying in English skies.

- The Red Arrows' colored wakes mix in an apparently casual manner during a crossover figure executed with precise timing.

638 and 639 • Almost all the acrobatic squads propose a close crossover in their programs, a spectacular, daring but technically safe figure.

640-641 • Two impressive maneuvers, performed by a duo, create suggestive wakes in the colors of the Royal Air Force.

U.S.A.

642 • The Thunderbirds, America's aeronautic squad, perform a nose-up in perfect
formation during the Daytona Airshow 2003, Florida.

643 • The classic "Bomb" opening interpreted by the Blue Angels, the U.S. Marines' squad.

644 • A tight passage on the right wing for these four F-16C Thunderbirds during the 2003 Daytona Airshow.

645 • The "Thunderbirds" perform for the public at Ft. Lauderdale (Florida) in 2003.

646-647 • Very close, the four USAF jets move in perfect synchrony.

648 • The positions of the earth and sky are relative for these Blue Angel pilots in this alternation of straight and upside down flight.

649 • The Blue Angels troop fly Boeing's F/A-18 Hornet fighters, the same aircraft that are used on aircraft carriers.

650 • The two Blue Angels soloists are photographed as they pass each other just a few feet apart.

651 • A transformation in a dive is performed for the public at the Ft. Lauderdale, Airshow, 2004.

652-653 • A Blue Angels' classic is the "mirror" figure: two aircraft with undercarriage, flap and landing hook extended, fly as close as 10 ft (3 m) to each other.

654 • • The "upside down mirror," with landing gear extended and aircraft very close to each other, entails enormous technical difficulty.

655 • The camera lens creates an optical effect that makes the four F/ A-18 Hornets seem like one aircraft.

Canada

656 • Canada's Snowbird squad members climb into the sky, maintaining a difficult formation.

657 • The Snowbirds perform the "diamond" at the U.S.A.F. base at Nellis, Nevada.

658-659 • The Snowbirds' nine CT-114 Tutor trainers captured while the squad designs a knot in the skies over Abbotsford, British Columbia, Canada.

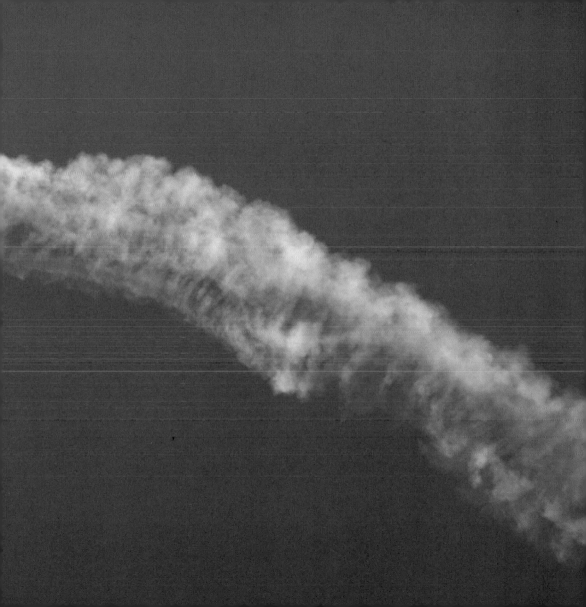

Chile

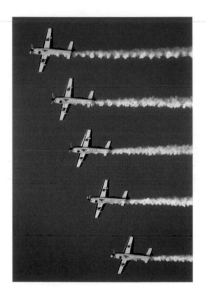

660 ● Chile's *Halcones* squad photographed during a "wing" passage over the U.S.A.F base at Nellis, Nevada, during the Golden Air Tattoo, 1997.

661 ● Here the "Extra 300" squad of Chile's *Halcones* performs a dynamic "break" in propeller aircraft.

Brasil

662 • The six Embraer EMB.312 Tucano of the Brazil's Esquadrilha de Fumaca in the sky over Abbotsford, Canada.

663 • The four Tucano of the brasilian troop "Esquadrilha de Fumaca" are trainers of turbopropeller propulsion.

● The Esquadrilha de Fumaca, flying turbotprops, demonstrate a cross over in the "T" formation and the opening phase of the "Bomb."

INTO THE NIGHT

JASMINA TRIFONI

- The sun sets in the Swedish sky, creating a magnificent play of colors across the horizon.

INTRODUCTION Into the Night

Since antiquity, humans have feared natural events and given the planet's evolutions a
mysterious meaning or spiritual symbolism. They
have looked to the moon to establish calendars,
the stars to sail the seas, and even invented leg-
ends and gods to explain the rising and setting
sun in terms of a beginning and an end, birth and
death. Over the centuries, through scientific and
technological discoveries man has investigated
the different laws that regulate nature and its
subtle, fragile environmental bonds. Humans have
moved from a condition of fear to one of mastery
– but they have also been instilled with a sense of
responsible awareness. From the air we can ad-

INTRODUCTION Into the Night

MIRE SUNRISES AND SUNSETS ALIGNED WITH THE CLOUDS. PARTICULARLY IN THE TROPICS, WE ARE STRUCK BY THE SPLENDOR OF DAWNS AND DUSKS, DAILY MARVELS THAT ALLOW US TO SHARE IN THE BEAUTY OF CREATION, FILLING US WITH PRIDE THAT WE TOO ARE PART OF THIS WONDER. THE PALETTES OF THE SKY SEEM EXPRESSLY MADE FOR PAINTERS AND PHOTOGRAPHERS: AN EX-TRAORDINARY DAWN IN CUBA, WITH AN ORANGE STAR THAT SEEMS TO RISE FROM THE VERY DEPTHS OF THE OCEAN; SUNSET OVER NORWAY'S SPECTACULAR HUR-TIGRUTEN ROUTE DURING THE SEASON OF THE MIDNIGHT SUN, WHICH SEEMS TO DIP INTO THE SEA ONLY TO RISE AGAIN IMMEDIATELY WITH THE DAWN; THE RED SKY SHIM-MERING OVER THE SCENERY OF ARIZONA AND UTAH'S

Into the Night
Introduction

MONUMENT VALLEY; THE GLOAMING – THE EVOCATIVE DUSK – VIEWED FROM A CASTLE HOSTEL IN SCOTLAND, AS THE SUN'S LAST RAYS SEEM TO BREAK UP THE RIPPLED SURFACE OF A LOCH TO FADE INTO A TREELESS HILL; THE SHORT SUNSET AND TWILIGHT OF SALAR DE O'YUNI IN BOLIVIA WHERE, BECAUSE OF THE ALTITUDE, THE SKY TURNS TO COLORS IMPOSSIBLE TO DESCRIBE; THE PINK SKY OVER ULURU, A SITE SACRED TO THE ABORIGINES, AND THE MYSTICAL WAIT FOR DAYBREAK IN THE DEPTHS OF NIGHT. NIGHT SKIES INSTEAD HAVE THEIR OWN LIGHT AND NUANCES, FORBIDDING YET MAGICAL: RARELY IS DARKNESS SO INKY BLACK THAT IT DOES NOT LEAVE ROOM FOR OTHER COLORS.

• In mid-January, in Sweden, the sun rises at aproximately 8.30 in the morning, each day creating a new show of light and color.

672-673 • A wintry atmosphere reigns at Ruhenstein, in the Black Forest, one of the most evocative and admired places in Germany.

674-675 • The cold sea that bathes the Finnish coast often provides a near-mystical experience for visitors, especially when the first warm spring air creates incredible mirages.

676-677 • Immense rice-fields surround Vercelli, Italy. From March to October, when they are flooded, they make the region seem like a huge lagoon.

678-679 • The sun rises behind a promontory in the south of Spain, giving the sky an almost irridescent color.

680-681 ●
A luminous sunset
enflames Punta Arenas,
on the Magellan Strait.

682-683 ●
Met by a companion,
an elephant begins its
characteristic "dust
bath" under the
Botswana sky.

684-685 ● A group of
impala graze on the
savanna in the Masai-
Mara National Reserve,
in Kenya, at the first
light of dawn.

● Each autumn, during the migration between Europe and Africa, hundreds of species of birds rest in the Neusiedler See National Park, Austria.

688 • During the winter, thousands of Canada geese migrate towards Colorado to nest.

689 • The magnificent colors of the sky at sunset are reflected in Lake Hamilton, Florida.

690-691 • The brief tropical sunset falls over the Cambodian forest.

692-693 • At sunset, a warm, delicate light spreads over Anna Maria Island, Florida.

694-695 • Under enormous cloud banks in the sky over Namibia, Burchell zebras graze in Etosha National Park.

On winter days, the blue and pink shades of the Swedish sky become are more intense, creating unforgettable images.

● In just a few moments the daylight dies out along the coast of Borneo, where the sun sets at exactly the same time all year long.

700 • Among the great oceanic flyers, frigates with their long white wings cross the sky over the Galapagos.

701 • At sunset, groups of ducks rest in the bird and fauna reserve of Bosque del Apache, in New Mexico, whose aquatic habitat is the home for hundreds of species of birds.

● The light at sunset
creates unusual
shadows, leaving a
solitary tree and the
Provençal plains in
shade.

704 and 705 • During sunset, the sun's reflections create many contrasts, especially in the clouds at mid and high altitudes, the last to reflect the sun's rays when the earth is already immersed in darkness.

706-707 • Colorado, often struck by violent atmospheric phenomena such as tornadoes, has one of the most spectacular skies in the world, as shown in this photo of the recent passage of a storm.

708-709 ● In the Fijian Islands, the calm that follows the storm takes on incredible forms: in this case a high cumulonimbus cloud in the background projects its shadow on the other clouds.

710-711 ● A sunset on the Finnish coast is reflected in the placid waters of the sea.

712, 713 and 714-715 • The rainy season, between November and April is not the best time to enjoy Polynesia's sun, but the sight offered by the sky and clouds is unbeatable.

716-717 • A flock of marine birds fly into the sunset on the Laguna de Gallocanta, in Spain.

718-719 • Similar to a distant mirage, an atoll emerges in the light of the Polynesian sunset.

720-721 • Like the flames of an enormous fire, sun-reddened clouds above a Swedish forest announce the sunset.

722-723 • At sunset, the Gallocanta Laguna, in Spain, offers a view of the storks taking flight before nightfall.

724-725 • In the savanna of the Masai-Mara Reserve in Kenya, one of Africa's celebrated sunsets reveals itself in all its splendor.

726-727 • Finland, Land of Lakes, has the peculiarity of doubling the wonders of the sky in its numerous "mirrors" of water.

AUTHORS Biographies

■ MAURIZIO BATTELLO,

A photographer and free-lance journalist, Battello has always been interested in painting and photography; he loves to portray natural subjects and, above all, skies and clouds. During these past years he has organized various slide shows of his travels, individual and group art and photography exhibits, and also "alternative-location" presentations (in shops, public buildings, monuments and open-air locations). Many of his images have been published in nature and travel magazines and in art and local history books. For years he has portrayed skies and clouds all over the world and in every meteorological condition (his dream is to portray the *aurora borealis*). His images record natural events (storms, dawns, sunsets, bizarre effects) as well as artificial ones (chemical vapors, chimney plumes, etc.) illustrating the subtle boundary between earth and sky.

■ ARIEL BRUNNER,

An expert in the conservation of biodiversity and a specialist in the politics and legislation of the European Union, Brunner currently serves as the Agricultural Representative for Europe with Birdlife International, the major worldwide network of associations dedicated to the conservation of birdlife. In the past five years he has been active with LIPU (Italian League for Bird Protection), national representative of the IBA sector (Important Bird Area) and Rete Natura 2000, for the defense of endangered natural sites and for the application of community-based environmental directives in Italy. Since his adolescence, which he spent in Israel – a true ornithologist's paradise – Brunner has cultivated a passion for bird-watching.

■ LUCA MERCALLI

Currently the president of the Italian Meteorological Society and director of the meteorological magazine "Nimbus" since 1993, Mercalli is the author of 80 scientific publications and over 500 popular scientific articles for "Repubblica" and other magazines, including "Alp", "L'Alpe", "Rivista della Montagna". He has taught climatology and glaciology at Turin University and Polytechnic of Turin. Director of the

Meteorological Observatory at the College Carlo Alberto in Moncalieri, he is member of the scientific committee of the Club Alpin Français and the Italian section of the WWF. He coordinated the *Climatic Atlas of Valle d'Aosta* and has published *The Time has Come* and *Cows Can't Eat Cement*.

■ RICCARDO NICCOLI,

Journalist, writer, photographer and historical, well-known flying enthusiast. Niccoli has been publishing articles and photographs in specialized magazines since 1982. He founded the publishing house RN Publishing and is director of the *Coccarde Tricolori* yearbook and *Compagnie & Aeroporti*. Niccoli also works with numerous international magazines and publishing houses. For White Star he wrote the comprehensive, fully illustrated *History of Flight*.

■ CARLOS SOLITO,

Motivated by a passion for travel and photography, Solito compiles reports and photojournalistic services worldwide, preferring anthropological and landscape themes. A successful freelancer, Solito contributes articles and photographs to numerous tourist, travel, environmental, nature and adventure magazines. He collaborates in publishing tour guides with a number of well-known publishing companies. A fan of speleology, paragliding and outdoor sports, Solito is strongly attracted by mountains. He has also produced a series of illustrated multimedia products presenting the identity and traditions of southern Italy. For White Star he collaborated on the fully illustrated volume *Puglia*, highlighting the life of this land of farming, olive groves, and good living. When not traveling, Solito lives in Irpinia, in the Campania region of Italy.

■ JASMINA TRIFONI

A graduate in Political Sciences, Jasmina Trifoni became a journalist specializing in tourism, and as a professional (and passionate) traveler has undertaken extensive ethnocultural research trips to India, South-East Asia and the Middle East. She contributes to several leading national magazines and is currently a member of the editorial staff of the magazine "Meridiani".

PHOTO CREDITS

PHOTO CREDITS

A summer downpour obscures the horizon off Cuba's northern coast.